A BOOK OF SAINTS AND WON-
DERS PUT DOWN HERE BY LADY
GREGORY ACCORDING TO THE
OLD WRITINGS AND THE MEMORY
OF THE PEOPLE OF IRELAND

NEW YORK
CHARLES SCRIBNER'S SONS
153-157 FIFTH AVENUE
1907

PRINTED BY
HAZELL, WATSON AND VINEY, LD.,
LONDON AND AYLESBURY,
ENGLAND.

CONTENTS   Page
BOOK ONE
BRIGIT, THE MARY OF THE GAEL

Brigit in her Young Youth	1
Brigit in her Father's House	1
She Minds the Dairy	2
She Fills the Vessels	3
The Man that had Lost his Wife's Love	4
The Drying of Brigit's Cloak	5
The King of Leinster's Fox	5
Brigit Spreads her Cloak	6
The Leper who would be a King	7
The Lake of Milk	7
The Things Brigit wished for	7
The Son of Reading	8
The Fishes Honour her	9
A Hymn made for Brigit by Brennain or another	9
Brigit Helps the Mother of God	10
The First of February	11
A Hymn Brocan made for Brigit	12
Her Care for Leinster	13
She Remembers the Poor	13
The Boy that dreamed he would get his Health	15
The Water of the Well	15
The Binding	16

CONTENTS

BOOK TWO
COLUMCILLE, THE FRIEND OF THE ANGELS OF GOD

The Golden Moon	17
He learns his Letters	18
His Helpers the Angels	18
Doire the Plain of the Oakwood	21
A Praise he made of Doire and he going over the Sea	21
Columcille's little Kinsman	24
His Farewell to Aran	25
The Island of Hii	28
The Crane from Ireland	29
Ireland was more to him than any other Place	30
The Poor Man and the Stake	31
The Nettle Broth	34
The Cranes of Druim Ceta	35
His Strange Visitor	36
The Breaking of Columcille's Guarantee	38
The Voyage of Snedgus	42
A Hymn Columcille made and he going a Journey	47
The Ladder of Glass	50
Columcille keeps the Feast of Pentecost	50
How the News was brought to Ireland	52
Forgaill's Lament	53
Columcille's Burying Place	56
Columcille's Valley	57

CONTENTS

BOOK THREE
BLESSED PATRICK OF THE BELLS

The Four Households	59
He gets his Freedom	59
The Man and Woman that were always Young	60
Patrick goes back to Ireland	61
The Deer's Cry	62
Patrick and the Big Men	64
The Hidden Well of Usnach	67
Patrick and Cascorach the Musician	68
Patrick's Farewell to Caoilte	72
Bodb Dearg's Daughter	73
Ethne the Beautiful and Fedelm the Rosy-Red	76
The Soul and the Body	78
Patrick's Rush Candles	78
His Church at Ardmacha	79
He is Waked by the Angels	79

BOOK FOUR
THE VOYAGE OF MAELDUNE

The Queen's Foster-Son	81
The Little Bald Islands	84
The Island of Ants	86
The Island of Birds	86
The Beast that was like a Horse	87
The Demon Riders	87
A House of Plenty	89

CONTENTS

The Apple Rod	89
The Whirling Beast	90
The Wicked Horses	91
The Fiery Pigs	91
The Little Cat	93
The War of Colours	95
The Weighty Calves	96
The Mill	97
The Island of Keening	97
The Four-Fenced Island	98
The Woman with the Pail	99
The Sound like Psalms	102
The Sod from Ireland	102
The Well of Nourishment	103
The Smiths at the Forge	104
The Very Clear Sea	105
The Sea like a Mist	106
The Pelting with Nuts	106
The Salmon Stream	107
The Silver-Meshed Net	108
The Door under Locks	109
The Ball of Thread	109
The Salley Trees	113
The Bird that got back its Youth	114
The Laughing People	117
The Fire-Walled Island	118
The Covetous Cook	118
The Bird from Ireland	124

CONTENTS

BOOK FIVE
GREAT WONDERS OF THE OLDEN TIME

Blessed Ciaran and his Scholars	127
His Kindness is living yet	129
Blessed Cellach's Lament	130
The Wolf's Prophecy	131
Liban the Sea Woman	133
The Priest and the Bees	136
The Hymn of Molling's Guest	137
Tuan, Son of Cairell	140
Fintain's Yew Tree	146
How Conchubar the High King died for Christ	147
The Wonders told by Philip the Apostle that was called the Ever-Living Tongue	149
The Seven Heavens	150
The Secrets of the Sea	151
Four of the World's Wells	152
The Four Precious Stones	153
The Four Trees that have a Life like the Angels	154
The Journey of the Sun	156
The Nature of the Stars	158
The High Ever-Living Birds	158
Four of the Strange Races of Mankind	160
The Valley of Pain	161

CONTENTS

The Cloud of Witnesses	163
A Praise of Caillen and his Blessed Death	164
The Calling of Martin the Miller	167
Martin and the Grass-Corn	167
The Birth of Colman of Aidhne	168
His Home in Burren	170
The Little Lad and the Birds	170
The Little Lad in the Well	171
Colman helps a Farmer	171
He shows Respect for Respect	172
A Very Good Well	172
Marbhan's Hymn of Content	172
Guaire, the Helper of the Poor	174
His Kindness to the Bush	175
The Making of the Harp	176
Mochae and the Bird	177
The Priest that was called Mad	179
The Old Woman of Beare	181

BOOK SIX
THE VOYAGE OF BRENDAN

His Vision of the Land of Promise	185
The News of the Hidden Country	185
The Beginning of Brendan's Search	188
The Very Comely Hound	189
The Island of Sheep	189
Jasconye the Fish	190
The Paradise of Birds	191

CONTENTS

The Silent Brotherhood	193
The Feast of the Resurrection	197
The Bird's Foretelling	197
The Dangers of the Sea	198
A Border of Hell	201
A Most Wretched Ghost	202
Paul the Hermit	205
A Lucky Journey	206
The Land of Promise	207
Brendan's Home-coming	208
Note	210

SAINTS AND WONDERS
BOOK ONE:
BRIGIT, THE MARY OF THE GAEL

BRIGIT IN HER YOUNG YOUTH Now as to Brigit she was born at sunrise on the first day of the spring, of a bondwoman of Connacht. And it was angels that baptized her and that gave her the name of Brigit, that is a Fiery Arrow. She grew up to be a serving girl the same as her mother. And all the food she used was the milk of a white red-eared cow that was set apart for her by a druid. And everything she put her hand to used to increase, and it was she wove the first piece of cloth in Ireland, and she put the white threads in the loom that have a power of healing in them to this day. She bettered the sheep and she satisfied the birds and she fed the poor.

BRIGIT IN HER FATHER'S HOUSE And when she grew to be strong and to have good courage she went to her father Dubthach's house in Munster and stopped with him there. And one time there came some high person to the house, and food was made ready for him and for his people; and five pieces of bacon were given to Brigit, to boil them. But there came into the house a very hungry miserable hound,

BOOK ONE: BRIGIT, THE

and she gave him out of pity a piece of the bacon. And when the hound was not satisfied with that she gave him another piece. Then Dubthach came and he asked Brigit were the pieces of bacon ready; and she bade him count them and he counted them, and the whole of the five pieces were there, not one of them missing. But the high guest that was there and that Brigit had thought to be asleep had seen all, and he told her father all that happened. And he and the people that were with him did not eat that meat, for they were not worthy of it, but it was given to the poor and to the wretched.

SHE MINDS THE DAIRY   After that Brigit went to visit her mother that was in bondage to a druid of Connacht. And it is the way she was at that time, at a grass-farm of the mountains having on it twelve cows, and she gathering butter. And there was sickness on her, and Brigit cared her and took charge of the whole place. And the churning she made, she used to divide it first into twelve parts in honour of the twelve apostles of our Lord; and the thirteenth part she would make bigger than the rest, to the honour of Christ, and that part she would give to strangers and to the poor. And the serving

MARY OF THE GAEL

boy wondered to see her doing that, but it is what she used to say: 'It is in the name of Christ I feed the poor; for Christ is in the body of every poor man.'

SHE FILLS THE VESSELS   One time the serving boy went to the druid's house, and they asked was the girl minding the dairy well. And he said 'I am thankful, and the calves are fat;' for he dared not say anything against the girl, and she not there. But the druid got word of what she was doing, and he came to visit the farm, and his wife along with him; and the cows were doing well, and the calves were fat. Then they went into the dairy, having with them a vessel eighteen hands in height. And Brigit bade them welcome and washed their feet, and made ready food for them, and after that they bade her fill up the vessel with butter. And she had but a churning and a half for them, and she went into the kitchen where it was stored and it is what she said:

'O my High Prince who can do all these things, this is not a forbidden asking; bless my kitchen with thy right hand!

' My kitchen, the kitchen of the white Lord; a kitchen that was blessed by my King; a kitchen where there is butter.

BOOK ONE: BRIGIT, THE

'My Friend is coming, the Son of Mary; it is he blessed my kitchen; the Prince of the world comes to this place; that there may be plenty with him!' After she had made that hymn she brought the half of the churning from the place where it was stored; and the druid's wife mocked at her and said 'It is good filling for a large vessel this much is!' 'Fill your vessel' said Brigit, 'and God will add something to it.' And she was going back to her kitchen and bringing half a churning every time and saying every time a verse of those verses. And if all the vessels of the men of Munster had been brought to her she would have filled the whole of them.

THE MAN THAT HAD LOST HIS WIFE'S LOVE

Brigit would give herself to no man in marriage but she took the veil and after that she did great wonders. There came to her one time a man making his complaint that his wife would not sleep with him but was leaving him, and he came asking a spell from Brigit that would bring back her love. And Brigit blessed water for him, and it is what she said: 'Bring that water into your house, and put it in the food and in the drink and on the bed.' And after he had done that, his wife gave him great love, so that

MARY OF THE GAEL

she could not be as far as the other side of the house from him, but was always at his hand. And one day he set out on a journey, leaving the wife in her sleep, and as soon as she awoke from her sleep she rose up and followed after her man till she saw him, and there was a strip of the sea between them. And she called out to him and it is what she said, that if he would not come back to her, she would go into the sea that was between them.

THE DRYING OF BRIGIT'S CLOAK One time Brennain, saint of the Gael, came from the west to Brigit, to the plain of the Life, for he wondered at the great name she had for doing miracles and wonders. And Brigit came in from her sheep to welcome him, and as she came into the house she laid her cloak that was wet on the rays of the sun, and they held it up the same as hooks. Then Brennain bade his serving lad to put his cloak on the sun rays in the same way, and he put it on them, but twice it fell from them. Then Brennain himself put it on them the third time, and there was anger on him, and that time it stopped on the rays.

THE KING OF LEINSTER'S FOX One time there was a man of her household cutting firing, and it chanced to him to kill

BOOK ONE: BRIGIT, THE

a pet fox belonging to the King of Leinster, and the King had him made prisoner. But Brigit called the fox out of the wood, and he came and was at his tricks and his games for the King and his people at Brigit's bidding. And when he had done his tricks he went away safe through the wood, and the army of Leinster, footmen and horsemen and hounds, after him.

BRIGIT SPREADS HER CLOAK When she was a poor girl she was minding her cow one time at the Curragh of Lifé, and she had no place to feed it but the side of the road. And a rich man that owned the land came by and saw her and he said 'How much land would it take to give grass to the cow?' 'As much as my cloak would cover' said she. 'I will give that' said the rich man. She laid down her cloak then, and it was spreading out miles and miles on every side. But there was a silly old woman passing by and she said 'If that cloak goes on spreading, all Ireland will be free;' and with that the cloak stopped and spread no more. And Brigit held that land through her lifetime, and it never had rent on it since, but the English Government have taken it now and have put barracks upon it. It is a pity the old woman spoke that time.

MARY OF THE GAEL

She did not know Brigit to be better than any other one.

THE LEPER WHO WOULD BE A KING A leper came one time to Brigit, asking a cow. And Brigit said 'Would you sooner have a cow or be healed of your disease?' 'I would sooner be healed' he said 'than to have the sway over the whole world. For every sound man is a king' he said. Then Brigit prayed to God; and the leper was healed, and served her afterwards.

THE LAKE OF MILK The Seven Bishops came to her in a place she had in the north of Kildare, and she asked her cook Blathnet had she any food, and she said she had not. And Brigit was ashamed, being as she was without food before those holy men, and she prayed hard to the Lord. Then angels came and bade her to milk the cows for the third time that day. So she milked them herself, and they filled the pails with the milk, and they would have filled all the vessels of the whole of Leinster. And the milk overflowed the vessels till it made a lake that is called the Lake of Milk to this day.

THE THINGS BRIGIT WISHED FOR These were the wishes of Brigit: 'I would wish a great lake of ale for the King

BOOK ONE: BRIGIT, THE

of Kings; I would wish the family of Heaven to be drinking it through life and time.

'I would wish the men of Heaven in my own house; I would wish vessels of peace to be giving to them.

'I would wish vessels full of alms to be giving away; I would wish ridges of mercy for peace-making.

'I would wish joy to be in their drinking; I would wish Jesus to be here among them.

'I would wish the three Marys of great name; I would wish the people of Heaven from every side.

'I would wish to be a rent-payer to the Prince; the way if I was in trouble he would give me a good blessing.'

Whatever, now, Brigit would ask of the Lord, he would give it to her on the moment. And it is what her desire was, to satisfy the poor, to banish every hardship, and to save every sorrowful man.

THE SON OF READING One time she was minding her sheep on the Curragh, and she saw a son of reading running past her. 'What is it makes you so uneasy?' she said 'and what is it you are looking for?' 'It is to Heaven I am running, woman of the veil' said the scholar. 'The Virgin's Son knows he

MARY OF THE GAEL

is happy that makes that journey' said Brigit. 'And pray to God to make it easy for myself to go there' she said. 'I have no time' said he; 'for the gates of Heaven are open now, and I am in dread they might be shut against me. And as you are hindering me' he said 'pray to the Master to make it easy for me to go there, and I will pray him to make it easy for you.' Then they said 'Our Father' together, & he was religious from that out, and it was he gave her absolution at the last. And it is by reason of him that the whole of the sons of learning of the world are with Brigit.

THE FISHES HONOUR HER   Brennain came to Brigit one time to ask why was it the beasts of the sea gave honour to her more than to the rest of the saints. Then they made their confession to each other, and Brennain said after that 'In my opinion, girl, it is right the beasts are when they honour you above ourselves.'

A HYMN MADE FOR BRIGIT BY BRENNAIN OR ANOTHER   'Brigit, excellent woman; sudden flame; may the bright fiery sun bring us to the lasting kingdom.

'May Brigit save us beyond troops of demons;

BOOK ONE: BRIGIT, THE

may she break before us the battles of every death.

'May she do away with the rent sin has put on us; the blossomed branch; the Mother of Jesus; the dear young woman greatly looked up to. That I may be safe in every place with my saint of Leinster!'

BRIGIT HELPS THE MOTHER OF GOD There was a poor man, and a poor woman, living in an ancient place in Ireland, a sort of a wilderness. The man used to be wishing for a son that would be a help to him with the work, but the woman used to say nothing, because she was good. They had a baby at last, but it was a girl, and the man was sorry and he said 'We will always be poor now.' But the woman said, for it was showed to her at that time, 'This child will be the Mother of God.' The girl grew up in that ancient place, and one day she was sitting at the door, and our Saviour sent One to her that said 'Would you wish to be the Mother of God?' 'I would wish it' said she. And on the minute, as she said that, the Saviour went into her as a child. The Messenger took her with him then, and he put beautiful clothing on her, and she turned to be so beautiful that all the people followed

MARY OF THE GAEL

them, crowding to see the two beautiful people that were passing by. They met then with Brigit, and the Mother of God said to her, 'What can we do to make these crowds leave following us?' 'I will do that for you' said Brigit 'for I will show them a greater wonder.' She went into a house then and brought out a harrow and held it up over her head, and everyone of the pins gave out a flame like a candle; and all the people turned back to look at the shining harrow that was such a great wonder. And it is because of that the harrow is blessed since that time. The Mother of God asked her then what would she do for her as a reward. 'Put my day before your own day' said Brigit. So she did that, and Saint Brigit's day is kept before her own day ever since. And there are some say Brigit fostered the Holy Child, and kept an account of every drop of blood he lost through his lifetime, and anyway she was always going about with the Mother of God.

THE FIRST OF FEBRUARY And from that time to this the housekeepers have a rhyme to say on Saint Brigit's day, bidding them to bring out a firkin of butter and to divide it among the working boys. For she

BOOK ONE: BRIGIT, THE

was good always, and it was her desire to feed the poor, to do away with every hardship, to be gentle to every misery. And it is on her day the first of the birds begin to make their nests, and the blessed Crosses are made with straw and are put up in the thatch; for the death of the year is done with and the birthday of the year is come. And it is what the Gael of Scotland say in a verse:
'Brigit put her finger in the river on the feast day of Brigit, and away went the hatching-mother of the cold.
'She washed the palms of her hands in the river on the day of the feast of Patrick, and away went the birth-mother of the cold.'

A HYMN BROCAN MADE FOR BRIGIT 'Victorious Brigit did not love the world; the spending of the world was not dear to her; a wonderful ladder for the people to climb to the kingdom of the Son of Mary.
'A wild boar came among her swine; he hunted the wild pigs to the north; Brigit blessed him with her staff, that he made his dwelling with her own herd.
'She was open in all her doings; she was only Mother of the great King's Son; she blessed the frightened bird till she played with it in her hand.

MARY OF THE GAEL

'Before going with angels to the battle let us go running to the church; to remember the Lord is better than any poem. Victorious Brigit did not love the world.'

HER CARE FOR LEINSTER On the day of the battle of Almhuin, Brigit was seen over the men of Leinster, and Columcille was seen over the Ua Neill; and it was the men of Leinster won that battle. And a long time after that again, when Strongbow that had brought great trouble into Ireland and that was promised the kingdom of Leinster was near his end, he cried out from his bed that he saw Brigit of the Gael, and that it was she herself was bringing him to his death.

SHE REMEMBERS THE POOR But if Brigit belonged to the east, it is not in the west she is forgotten, and the people of Burren and of Corcomruadh and Kinvara go every year to her blessed well that is near the sea, praying and remembering her. And in that well there is a little fish that is seen every seven years, and whoever sees that fish is cured of every disease. And there is a woman living yet that is poor and old and that saw that blessed fish, and this is the way she tells the story: 'I had a pearl in my eye one time, and I went to Saint Brigit's well on the cliffs.

BOOK ONE: BRIGIT, THE

Scores of people there were in it, looking for cures, and some got them and some did not get them. And I went down the four steps to the well and I was looking into it, and I saw a little fish no longer than your finger coming from a stone under the water. Three spots it had on the one side and three on the other side, red spots and a little green with the red, and it was very civil coming hither to me and very pleasant wagging its tail. And it stopped and looked up at me and gave three wags of its back, and walked off again and went in under the stone.

'And I said to a woman that was near me that I saw the little fish, and she began to call out and to say there were many coming with cars and with horses for a month past and none of them saw it at all. And she proved me, asking had it spots, and I said it had, three on the one side and three on the other side. 'That is it' she said. And within three days I had the sight of my eye again. It was surely Saint Brigit I saw that time; who else would it be? And you would know by the look of it that it was no common fish. Very civil it was, and nice and loughy, and no one else saw it at all. Did I say more prayers than the rest? Not a prayer. I was young in those days. I

MARY OF THE GAEL

suppose she took a liking to me, maybe because of my name being Brigit the same as her own.'

THE BOY THAT DREAMED HE WOULD GET HIS HEALTH

There was a beggar boy used to be in Burren, that was very simple like and had no health, and if he would walk as much as a few perches it is likely he would fall on the road. And he dreamed twice that he went to Saint Brigit's blessed well upon the cliffs and that he found his health there. So he set out to go to the well, and when he came to it he fell in and he was drowned. Very simple he was and innocent and without sin. It is likely it is in heaven he is at this time.

THE WATER OF THE WELL

And there is a woman in Burren now is grateful to Saint Brigit, for 'I brought my little girl that was not four years old' she says 'to Saint Brigit's well on the cliffs, where she was ailing and pining away. I brought her as far as the doctors in Gort and they could do nothing for her and then I promised to go to Saint Brigit's well, and from the time I made that promise she got better. And I saw the little fish when I brought her there; and she grew to be as strong a girl as ever went to America. I made

BOOK ONE

a promise to go to the well every year after that, and so I do, of a Garlic Sunday, that is the last Sunday in July. And I brought a bottle of water from it last year and it is as cold as amber yet.'

THE BINDING   And when the people are covering up a red sod under the ashes in the night time to spare the seed of the fire for the morning, they think upon Brigit the Fiery Arrow and it is what they do be saying: 'I save this fire as Christ saved everyone; Brigit beneath it, the Son of Mary within it; let the three angels having most power in the court of grace be keeping this house and the people of this house and sheltering them until the dawn of day.' For it is what Brigit had a mind for; lasting goodness that was not hidden; minding sheep and rising early; hospitality towards good men. It is she keeps everyone that is in straits and in dangers; it is she puts down sicknesses; it is she quiets the voice of the waves and the anger of the great sea. She is the queen of the south; she is the mother of the flocks; she is the Mary of the Gael.

BOOK TWO:
COLUMCILLE, THE FRIEND OF THE ANGELS OF GOD

THE GOLDEN MOON It is noble indeed was the race of Columcille as to this world; and he had a right through his blood to the kingship of Ireland but he put it from him for the sake of God. One time Fintain had a vision, and he saw in the vision two moons that rose up from Cluan Eraird, the one a silver moon and the other a golden moon. The golden moon went on towards the north till it lightened Scotland and the northern part of Ireland; and the silver moon went on till it stopped by the Sionnan and lightened the middle part of Ireland. Columcille now was the golden moon with his high race and his wisdom; and Ciaran was the silver moon with the brightness of his virtues and his pleasant ways. And the place where he was born was Gortan in the north; and it was on a Thursday he was born, that has from that time been a lucky day. And indeed it was a wonderful child was born that day, Columcille son of Fedilmid son of Fergus son of Connall Gulban son of Niall of the Nine Hostages. There was not a man of higher race or of greater name born of the Gael. And he was brought for baptism to Cruithnechan the

BOOK TWO: COLUMCILLE, THE

noble priest; and it was he fostered him afterwards at the bidding of an angel; and it was angels that gave him his name.

HE LEARNS HIS LETTERS   And when the time for reading came to him, the priest went to a knowledgeable man that was in the country and asked him when would it be right for the little lad to begin. And when the knowledgeable man had looked at the sky he said 'Write out the letters for him now.' So the letters were written out upon a cake, and it is the way Columcille ate the cake, one part to the east of the water and the other part to the west of the water. And the knowledgeable man said then through his prophecy 'It is the same way the sway of this young lad will be, one half to the east of the sea in Scotland, and the other half to the west of the sea in Ireland.'

HIS HELPERS THE ANGELS   After he left his fosterer he went from place to place for a while until he came to where Fintain was at Cluan Eraird, and he built a cabin there. And at that time every one of the twelve saints of Ireland used to take his turn to grind meal in a quern through the night; but it was an angel of God in heaven used to grind for Columcille. That was the honour the

FRIEND OF THE ANGELS OF GOD

Lord gave him because of the nobleness of his race beyond the others. For as to angels it is often they were about him, and it is often they helped him from the beginning of his life until the end. One time he was put out of the brotherhood for no just cause, and the brothers were all gathered together at Tailltin holding a meeting against him, and he himself came to the meeting. And Brenden that was there rose up when he saw him coming and when he came near he kissed him with great respect. Some of the old men in the gathering took Brenden on one side then and they were faulting him and saying 'Why did you rise up before a man that has been put out of the brotherhood and why did you kiss him?' And it is what Brenden said 'If you had seen today what the Lord thought fit to show to me, you would not have dishonoured him that God holds in such honour.' 'What was it you saw?' said they. 'It is what I saw' said Brenden 'a very bright pillar with fiery hair about it going before this man that you make little of; and the company I saw travelling over the plain with him were the angels of God.' One night a very beautiful young man in shining clothes came to Columcille in the night time and said 'God be with you, and

BOOK TWO: COLUMCILLE, THE

be strong now and steadfast, for God has sent me to keep you for ever and always from all the sin of the world.' But Columcille was afraid, and asked him who he was. 'I am Axal' he said 'that is a helper, an angel of the Lord; and it is to help you and to protect you from every danger and trouble of the world I am come.' And from that time there were many angels used to be coming to his help, but it is likely Axal was the one that was always at hand. One time Columcille was sitting in his little cell, and he writing, and of a sudden his looks changed and he called out 'Help! help!' Then two of the brothers that were at the door asked the cause of that cry. And Columcille told them that of a sudden he had seen one of the brothers falling from the highest point of a high house that was being built in Doire. 'And I bade the angel of the Lord' he said 'that was just now standing among you to go to his relief. And with all the land and sea that lay between' he said 'the angel that had but left us as he began to fall was there in time to support him before he reached the ground, so that there was no hurt or bruise upon him at all. And that was wonderful help' he said 'that could be given so very quickly as that.'

FRIEND OF THE ANGELS OF GOD

DOIRE THE PLAIN OF THE OAKWOOD Aedh King of Ireland gave up the dun he had in Doire to Columcille and he made his dwelling there. And he had so great a love for Doire, and the cutting of the oak trees went so greatly against him, that he could not find a place for his church the time he was building it that would let the front of it be to the east, and it is its side was turned to the east. And he left it upon those that came after him not to cut a tree that fell of itself or was blown down by the wind in that place to the end of nine days, and then to share it between the people of the townland, bad and good, a third of it to the great house and a tenth to be given to the poor. And he put a verse in a hymn after he was gone away to Scotland that shows there was nothing worse to him than the cutting of that oakwood:

'Though there is fear on me of death and of hell, I will not hide it that I have more fear of the sound of an axe over in Doire.'

A PRAISE HE MADE OF DOIRE AND HE GOING OVER THE SEA 'It is delightful to be on Beinn Edair before going over the white sea; the beating of the waves against its wall; the bareness of its border and its strand.

BOOK TWO: COLUMCILLE, THE

'It is great is the swiftness of my currach and its back turned to Doire; it is a fret to me my journey over the high sea, travelling to Scotland of the ravens.

'My foot in my sweet-sounding currach; my sorrowful heart pleading. It is a weak man that is not a leader; all that are without knowledge are blind altogether.

'There is a grey eye that is looking back upon Ireland; it will never see from day to day the men or the women of Ireland. I stretch my sight over the salt waters from the strong oaken planks; there is a big tear in my eye when I look back on Ireland; my mind is set upon Ireland, on Loch Lene of Magh Line; on the country of the men of Ulster; on smooth Munster and on Meath.

'It is plentiful in the east are tall fighting men; plentiful the troubles and the sicknesses; plentiful the men with scanty clothes; plentiful the hard jealous hearts.

'Plentiful in the west are the apples; plentiful the kings & the makings of kings; plentiful the wholesome sloes; plentiful the oaks with acorns.

'Sweetvoiced her clerks; sweetvoiced her birds; her young men gentle her old men wise;

FRIEND OF THE ANGELS OF GOD

her great men are good to look at; her women noble, of good rearing.

'Take my blessing with you beautiful boy, my blessing and my benediction; the half of it for Ireland seven times over; the other half once for Scotland. Take my blessing over the sea to the nobles of the island of the Gael; let them not give heed to their enemy's words, or to his threat of harming them.

'Take my blessing with you to the west; my heart is broken in my body. If death should overtake me suddenly it is through great love of the Gael.

'Gael, Gael, dear dear name, my one shout and my call! Dear is soft haired Cuimin, dear are Caindech and Comgall.

'If I had the whole of Scotland from the middle out to the borders I would sooner have a place and a house in the middle of pleasant Doire.

'It is the reason I love Doire, for its quietness for its purity; it is quite full of white angels from the one end to the other.

'It is the reason I love Doire, for its quietness for its purity; quite full of white angels is every leaf of the oaks of Doire.

'My Doire my little oakwood, my dwelling

BOOK TWO: COLUMCILLE, THE

and my white cell; O living God in heaven, it is a pity for him that harms it!

'Dear are Durrow and Doire; dear is Rathboth in its whiteness; dear is Druimhome of delicate fruits; dear are Sord and Cenacles.

'Dear to my heart in the west Druimcliab at the strand of Culcinne; to see white Loch Febhail, the shape of its harbour is delightful.

'Delightful is that and delightful is the sea where the gulls are crying; going a long way from Doire it is quiet and it is delightful!'

COLUMCILLE'S LITTLE KINSMAN Baothan that was afterwards a saint of the Gael was of the kindred of Columcille, and it was Columcille sent him when he was a little lad to be taught by Saint Colman Ela. But although Baothan had good wits enough his memory failed him, and it was hard for him to keep in mind what his master taught him. And it happened one day that Colman was vexed with him at his task and struck him. Then Baothan went away into the wood to hide himself and to avoid his tasks, and while he was there he saw a man alone and he building a house; and according as he came to the end of weaving one rod into the wall he would set the head of another to it, and so he worked on from rod to rod setting one

FRIEND OF THE ANGELS OF GOD

only at a time. And that seemed very tedious to the young lad till he saw the wall rising as he watched; and he said to himself then 'If I had worked at my learning as this man works at his building it is likely I might be a scholar now.' Then a shower of rain fell and he took shelter from it under an oak tree and he saw a drop of the rain falling from a leaf of the tree on one spot, and he pressed his heel on that spot and made a little hollow, and it was not long till it was filled by the dropping of the one drop. And Baothan said then 'If I had worked at my task and my learning even little by little like that drop without doubt I would be a scholar now. And I make my vow' he said 'that from this out to my life's end I will never give up my learning however hard it may be to me.'

HIS FAREWELL TO ARAN   Columcille made a round of the whole of Ireland & he sowed the faith and did what he had to do. And before he went to Scotland he stopped in Aran of the Saints for a while, and there is a spot in the island where he used to be walking and that is always green to this day. And when he left Aran he made this complaint:

'A farewell from me to Aran; a sorrowful

BOOK TWO: COLUMCILLE, THE

farewell as I think; I myself sent eastward to Hii, and the sea between it and Aran.

'A farewell from me to Aran; it is it that vexes my heart; I not to be westward on her waves among troops of the saints of heaven.

'A farewell from me to Aran; my faithful heart is vexed; it is a lasting leavetaking; Och! this parting is not of my will.

'A farewell from me to Aran; it is that is the sorrowful parting; she to be full of white angels and I without a lad in my currach.

'Och it is far, Ochone it is far I am put away from Aran in the west; sent out towards the hosts of Mona to visit the men of Scotland in the east.

'The Son of God, O the Son of God, it is He sent me out to Hii; it is He gave, great the profit, Aran as the dwelling-place of prayers and of teaching.

'Aran my sun, O Aran my sun, my affection is lying in her to the west; it is the same to be under her clean earth as under the earth of Paul and Peter.

'Aran my sun, O Aran my sun, my love is lying in her to the west; to be within the sound of her bell, it is the same thing as to be in happiness.

'Aran my sun, O Aran my sun, my love is

FRIEND OF THE ANGELS OF GOD

lying in her to the west; whoever goes under her clean earth, the eye of no bad thing will see him.

'Blessed Aran, O blessed Aran, it is a pity for anyone that is against Aran; it is what he will get on the head of it, shortening of life and the grave.

'Blessed Aran, O blessed Aran, it is a pity for him that is against Aran; wasting on his children and on his cattle; he himself in bad case at the end.

'Blessed Aran, O blessed Aran, it is a pity for anyone that is against you; angels coming down from Heaven to visit you every day of the week.

'Gabriel comes every Sunday as it is Christ gave the order; fifty angels, not weak the cause, putting a blessing on her Masses.

'Every Monday, O every Monday, Michael comes, great the advantage; thirty angels, good their behaviour, come blessing her churches.

'Every Tuesday, O every Tuesday, Raphael comes, of high power; to give a blessing on her houses attending on the prayers of Aran.

'Hard Wednesday, O hard Wednesday, Urial comes, great the advantage; he comes to bless three times over the high angelic churches.

BOOK TWO: COLUMCILLE, THE

'Every Thursday, O every Thursday, Sariel comes, great the advantage; dividing God's good increase from heaven on the bare stones.

'Every Friday, O every Friday, Ramael comes, his ranks with him; the way every eye is satisfied with white very bright angels.

'Mary comes, Mother of God, having her women in her keeping; angels are in their company; they bless Aran every Saturday.

'If there was no other life but listening to the angels of Aran, it would be better than any life under heaven to be hearing their talk together!'

THE ISLAND OF HII   And when he left Ireland for Scotland he did good service there; for it was he brought many of the men of Scotland from darkness to the light of belief and of good deeds. It was to the island of Hii he went first and when he reached to it he said to his people 'It would be well for us to put roots into the earth in this place. And there is leave for one of you' he said 'to go under the earth of this island to consecrate it.' Odhran rose up quickly then and it is what he said 'I am ready for that if you will take me.' 'You will get your reward for that Odhran' said Columcille 'for no asking will be granted to anyone at this place unless he

FRIEND OF THE ANGELS OF GOD

will ask it first of you.' Then Odhran joined the company of Heaven, and after that Columcille laid the foundation of his church. And he bade the brothers to have a mind prepared for red martyrdom and a mind strong and steadfast for white martyrdom; forgiveness from the heart to everyone; constant prayer for all that troubled them. 'And let you be as much in earnest saying the office for the dead' he said 'as if every one of the faithful dead was your own near friend.' But if it was in Hii he had his dwelling-place, he went every Thursday to Heaven at the call of the King of the Three Peoples.

THE CRANE FROM IRELAND One time when Columcille was living in the island of Hii he called to one of the brothers and said 'In the morning of the third day from this go down and wait on the shore to the west of the island, for at the ninth hour there will come a stranger, a crane from the north part of Ireland, that has been driven here and there by winds and it will lie down on the strand tired and worn out. And bring it into some neighbouring house' he said 'where it will get a welcome, and where you can be minding it and feeding it for three days and three nights. And when it is re-

BOOK TWO: COLUMCILLE, THE

freshed' he said 'with the three days' rest and has no mind to stay longer with us it will fly back to the pleasant part of Ireland it came from. And I give this bird to your special care' he said 'because it is from our own country it comes.' And the brother did as he bade him and tended the crane. And at the end of the third day the crane rose to a great height in the air and stopped for a little while marking out its path to its home. And then it went back across the sea to Ireland as straight as it could fly on a calm day. For Ireland was never out of Columcille's mind and it is what he used to say 'The Gael are more to me than all the rest of the men of the world.'

IRELAND WAS MORE TO HIM THAN ANY OTHER PLACE

Columcille made this hymn one time, praising Ireland:

'It would be delightful Son of my God, to travel over the waves of the rising flood; over Loch Neach, over Loch Febhail, beyond Beinn Eigne, the place we used to hear fitting music from the swans. The host of the gulls would make a welcome with their sleepy music if my currach the Red Dewy One should come to the harbour of joyous anger.

FRIEND OF THE ANGELS OF GOD

'I have my fill of riches if I thought it enough, wanting Ireland, in the strange country where I have chanced and I tired. It is a pity the journey that was put upon me O King of mysteries!

'It is happy the son of Dima is, he of the faithful church, when he is listening in Durrow to the desire of his mind; the sound of the wind against the elms; the laughter of the blackbird clapping his wings; to listen at break of day to the lowing of the cattle in Rigrencha, to listen at the brink of summer to the cry of the cuckoo from the tree.

'There are three things dearest to me on the whole of this peopled world, Doire and Doire-Ethne and Doire the high country of angels. My visit to Comgall, my feast with Cainnech, it is they were honey sweet to me. I have loved Ireland of the waters, all that is in it but its government.'

THE POOR MAN AND THE STAKE   There came to Columcille one time a poor man of Scotland that was in great misery and had no way of living. And when Columcille had given him all he had to give of alms he said to him 'Go now into that wood beyond and bring me a branch from it.' The poor man did as he bade him and brought the

BOOK TWO: COLUMCILLE, THE

branch and Columcille took it and made a sharp point on it and he gave it back to the poor man and he said 'Take good care of the stake and so long as you have it you will never be without plenty of venison in the house. But it will not harm men or cattle' he said 'but only wild creatures, beasts and fishes.' The poor man was well pleased when he heard that, and as he went home he fixed the stake in a lonely place where the wild creatures of the wood used to be going. And at the early light of the morrow he went to look at the stake and it is the way it was, a very large stag had fallen upon it and it had gone through him. And from that out not a day would pass but he would find a stag or a doe or some other wild creature fixed upon the stake the way his house was full of meat, and all that himself and his wife and his children could not use he would sell it to the neighbours. But after a while his wife said to him 'Take out that stake out of the ground, for if men or cattle should chance to fall upon it, yourself and myself and our children would be put to death or we would be led into bondage.' And it is not as a wise woman she spoke that time but as a woman that had lost her sense. 'That is a thing will not happen'

FRIEND OF THE ANGELS OF GOD

said the husband 'for when the holy man blessed the stake he said it would never harm men or cattle.' But for all that he did as his wife bade him and in his folly he took the stake out of the ground and put it against the wall. And not long after that, his house dog fell upon it and was killed. And his wife said to him then 'One of the children will be the next to fall upon it and to be killed.' So when she said that he took the stake out the house, and brought it to a very large wood and put it in the thickest of the scrub where as he thought no beast could be harmed by it. But when he came back next day what he saw was a deer that had fallen upon it and got its death. So he brought it away from there and thrust it in under the water by the edge of a river; and the next day he found on it a salmon so big that it is hardly he was able to lift it out of the river to bring it home. And that time he brought the stake up from the river and put it outside on the roof of his house. But it was not long till a crow got its death by it, where it was coming to pitch on the house. And upon that the foolish man giving in to the advice of his wife took down the stake from the roof and took an axe and cut it in a great many pieces and threw it in

BOOK TWO: COLUMCILLE, THE

the fire. And after doing that, he that had been rich fell into poverty again and it is well he had earned it. And all he had to do, and his wife and his children for the rest of their lives, was to fret after the stake the blessed man had given him, and that he himself had done away with.

THE NETTLE BROTH   One time he was making his rounds in Hii and he saw an old woman and she cutting nettles to boil down for food. 'What is the cause of that misery?' said Columcille. 'O dear father' she said 'I have one cow only and she is in calf, and this is what serves through the time of waiting.' When Columcille heard that, he made his mind up he would use no other thing than broth of nettles so long as his life would last. 'For if it is waiting for the one cow this woman is, in this great hunger' he said 'it would be more fitting for us to be in hunger; for it is a better thing we ourselves are waiting for, the everlasting kingdom.' And he said to his cook 'Bring me broth of nettles every night and bring no milk with it.' 'I will do that' said the cook. But it is what the cook did, he bored a hole through the stick he stirred the broth with, till it was like a pipe, & he used to pour the juice of meat

FRIEND OF THE ANGELS OF GOD

down through the pipe so that it was mixed with the broth. And that kept a good appearance on Columcille, and the brothers saw by his looks he was well nourished and they were talking about it among themselves. And when Columcille knew that he said 'That those that come after you may be always grumbling. And what is it you are giving me?' he said to the cook. 'You know well yourself' said the cook 'that if it does not come through the iron of the pot or through the stick the broth is mixed with, I know of no other thing in it but only nettles.' 'That there may be good luck and a good appearance to those that come after you for ever' said Columcille. And it is likely he took but nettles only after that, for he lost flesh till the track of his ribs used to be seen on the strand when he used to lie out there through the night time.

THE CRANES OF DRUIM CETA   Columcille went back one time to Ireland to the great gathering of Druim Ceta to bless the people, and to get leave for the troops of the poets that were being driven out for their burdensomeness, to stop in Ireland. For it is what he said, that the rewards they got were not lasting but their praises would last for

BOOK TWO: COLUMCILLE, THE

ever. Then Aedh King of Ireland gave leave for them to stop, but there was anger on him and on Conall his son, Columcille to have come to the gathering. And Conall stirred up the rabble of the gathering against Columcille's people that they made an attack on them and took some and wounded others. And when Columcille knew that, he put a curse on Conall and rang three times nine bells against him and took the kingship from him, and his reason & his wits. And when the Queen heard that, and she washing her flower-face at the time, she said to her serving maid 'Go to Aedh and say to him that if he shows respect to this crane-clerk I will not be peaceable towards himself.' And when Columcille was told that, it is what he said, that the Queen and her serving maid should be put into the shape of cranes of Druim Ceta from that day to the day of judgment, and she having one of her wings broken and but half a tail. And so it happened, and if they are not in it yet they were long enough in it, the two old cranes of Druim Ceta.

HIS STRANGE VISITOR   One time Columcille was at Carn Eolairg on Loch Febhail and there came a beautiful young man to him having a golden shoe upon his foot,

FRIEND OF THE ANGELS OF GOD

and whatever foot he would put down it is on it the shoe used to be. 'Where do you come from young man?' said Columcille. 'I am Mongan son of Fiachra' said the young man 'and I am come from countries unknown and countries known. And I am come' he said 'to compare my knowledge and wisdom with your own, and to know from you the place where knowledge & ignorance were born, the place where they die and the place of their burying.' 'A question to you' said Columcille, 'what used this loch we are looking at to be in the old time?' 'I know that' said the young man. 'It was yellow, it was blossoming, it was green, it was hilly, it was a place of drinking, it had silver in it and chariots. I went through it when I was a deer before deer, when I was a salmon, when I was a very strong seal, when I was a wild dog. When I was a man I bathed in it, I carried a yellow sail, a green sail, it drowned a red sail under blood, women called out to me. Though I do not know father or mother I speak with the living and the dead.' Then Columcille said to him 'What is there beneath those islands to the west of us?' And it is what the young man said: 'There are underneath them tuneful long-haired men; there are

BOOK TWO : COLUMCILLE, THE
well-shaped people both men and women; there are cattle, white, red-eared, their lowing is sweet; there are herds of deer, there are good horses; there are the two-headed, there are the three-headed, in Europe, in Asia, in an unknown green country from its border to its river mouth.' 'That is enough so far' said Columcille. And then he went apart with the young man to ask him the secrets of heaven and earth. And they were talking together from one hour on that day to the same hour on the next day, and Columcille's people were looking at them a long way off. And when the talk came to an end they saw the young man vanishing from them all of a minute, and it is not known where he went. And when they asked Columcille to give them news of his talk it is what he said, that he could not tell them one word of all he had heard; and he said it was a right thing for men not to be told of it.

THE BREAKING OF COLUMCILLE'S GUARANTEE   Fergal King of Ireland that was of the race of the Ua Neills of the north was gathering his people one time to go against the men of Leinster. And it was a long time they took coming together, for it is what every man that was called in

FRIEND OF THE ANGELS OF GOD

Conn's half of Ireland used to say: 'If Donnbo goes with the army I will go.' Donnbo now was the son of a widow-woman belonging to the men of Ross, and he had never gone away from his mother's house for one day or for one night only; and there was not one in all Ireland more comely or better in face and in shape than himself. He was the best at singing merry verses and telling royal stories of all in the whole world; the best to ready horses or to rivet spears or to plait hair; the best in quickness of mind and in generosity. And his mother would not let him go out at the king's bidding till she got the security of Columcille that he would come back to her in safety. So he went out with the king's army, and they went on till they came to Almhuin and there they made their camp. And it was then Fergal said to Donnbo 'Make mirth for us Donnbo, for you are the best of all the musicians of Ireland at pipes and at harps and at poems, and at the old stories and the royal stories of Ireland; and on the morning of tomorrow' he said 'we will give battle to the men of Leinster.' 'Och' said Donnbo 'I am not able to make sport for you this night or to do any of those things that you say. But wherever you may be on the night of to-

BOOK TWO: COLUMCILLE, THE

morrow' he said 'I will make amusement for you if I am living. And let the king's buffoon make sport for you to-night' he said. So Ua Maighlinne the king's buffoon was called and he began his stories of the battles and the triumphs of Leinster from the destruction of Dind Righ down to that time. And it was not much sleep they got that night because of their great dread of the men of Leinster, and because of a storm that arose; for that was the eve of the feast of Saint Finnain in the winter. The battle was fought the next morning & the men from the north were beaten, and nine thousand of them got their death, and Fergal the king among them. And Ua Maighlinne fell into the hands of one of the men of Leinster, and he bade him give his buffoon's roar, and he did that; and his head was cut off then, but the roar was heard in the air through the length of three nights and three days and it has stayed with the buffoons of Ireland to this day. And as to Donnbo, he lost his life defending the king, and his head was struck off, and the king's head. The same night now the men of Leinster were drinking wine and making merry, and every one telling the deeds he had done in the battle. And Murchad son of the king of

FRIEND OF THE ANGELS OF GOD

Leinster said 'I would give a good chariot and my own dress to any man that would go to the place of the battle and would bring me a token from it.' 'I will go' said a Munster man that was among them. So he put on his battle dress and went on, and when he came to the place where king Fergal's body was, he heard said as if in the air these words 'Here is a command to you from the King of the Seven Heavens; make music to-night for your master Fergal the king; though all of you have fallen here, pipers and trumpeters and harpers, let no terror or no weakness keep you from making music for Fergal.' Then the messenger heard the music of singers and trumpeters and pipers and harpers, all sorts of music he heard, and he never heard better before or after. And from a bunch of rushes near him he heard a very wild song, the sweetest of all the music of the world. He went towards the rushes then and a voice said from among them 'Do not come near me.' 'Who are you?' said the messenger. 'I am the head of Donnbo' it said 'and I was bound in a bond to make amusement for the king to-night, and do not hinder me.' 'Where is Fergal's body?' said the messenger. 'It is shining there before you' said the head. 'Let me bring you away along

BOOK TWO: COLUMCILLE, THE

with him' said the messenger, 'for it is yourself I would sooner bring away.' 'I would not wish any person to bring me away' said the head 'unless it might be Christ the Son of God. And give me the guarantee of Christ now that you will bring me back to my body again.' 'I will bring you surely' said the messenger. Then he went back to where the men of Leinster were drinking yet. 'Have you a token with you?' said Murchad. 'I have' said he 'the head of Donnbo.' 'Set it up on that post' said Murchad. Then they all knew it to be the head of Donnbo, and it is what they all said: 'It is a pity for you Donnbo, it is comely your face was! And make amusement for us to-night,' they said 'the same as you did yesterday for your lord.' Then he turned his face to the wall of the house the way it would be darker for him, and he raised his wild song, and it was the sweetest of all the music on the whole ridge of the world. And all the men of Leinster were crying and lamenting, with the sorrow and the softness of that song.

THE VOYAGE OF SNEDGUS   One time Snedgus and Mac Riaghta, clerks that were of the people of Columcille, got into their currach of their own will, and went out

FRIEND OF THE ANGELS OF GOD

over the sea on a pilgrimage, and they turned righthandways and the wind brought them north-westward into the outer ocean. And at the end of three days a great longing and a great thirst came upon them that they could not bear; and it was then Christ took pity on them and brought them to an island where there was a stream that had the taste of new milk, and they were satisfied with it. They gave thanks to God then and they said 'Let us leave our voyage to God, and let us put the oars in the boat.' And from that out they let the rudder alone and they put their oars in the boat. Then they were brought to another island having a silver paling over the middle of it, and a fish weir; and it is a plank of silver that weir was, and there were big salmon, every one the size of a bull-calf, leaping against the weir, and they were satisfied with them. After that they went to another island and in that island they found fighting-men having heads of cats on them. And there was one man of the Gael among them, and he came down to the strand and bade them welcome and he said 'A boat's crew of us came here, and there is not one left of it now but myself, for the rest of us were made an end of

BOOK TWO : COLUMCILLE, THE

by the strangers of this island.' He put provision into the boat for them then, and they left a blessing and took a blessing with them. After that the wind brought them to an island where there was a great tree, and beautiful birds in it; and on the top of the tree was a bird having a head of gold and wings of silver; and it told them stories of the beginning of the world & it told them of the birth of Christ from Mary Virgin, and of his baptism and his passion and his rising again; and it told news of the judgment. And then all the birds beat their sides with their wings till blood dropped from them, with the dread of the signs of the judgment, and it is a very precious thing that blood was. And the bird gave to the clerks a leaf of the leaves of that tree, and it is the size of the hide of a great ox that leaf was and neither leaf nor stem of that tree withers. And he bade them to put that leaf on Columcille's altar, and it is to Kells it was brought afterwards. It is sweet the music of those birds was, singing psalms & praising the Lord, for they were the birds of the plain of Heaven. Then they bade farewell to the birds, and they went on to a very fearful country where there were men having heads of dogs and

FRIEND OF THE ANGELS OF GOD

manes of cattle. And by order of God a clerk came to them out of the island to relieve them, for they were in a bad way for the want of food; and he gave them fish and wine and wheat. Then they went on till they came to a country where there were men having heads of pigs; and there were a great many reapers reaping the corn in the middle of the summer. And from that they went on in their boat, and sang their psalms and prayed to God, till they came to a country where there were people of the Gael; and the women of that island sang a strain to the clerks and it is sweet they thought it. And one of them said 'Sing on, for this is the music of Ireland.' 'Let us go to the house of the King of the island' said the women to them then, 'and you will get a welcome and good treatment.' So they went into the house, and the King gave a welcome to the clerks, and they rested themselves there and he asked them what was their race. 'We are of the men of Ireland' they said 'and of the people of Columcille.' 'What way is Ireland now?' said the King 'and how many of the sons of Domnall are living yet?' 'There are three sons of Domnall living, and Fiachna son of Domnall fell by the men of Ross and

BOOK TWO: COLUMCILLE, THE

for that deed two sixties of them were put out upon the sea.' 'It is true that story is' said the King; 'it is I myself killed the son of Domnall king of Teamhuir and we are the men were put out on the sea. And it is well that happened for us' he said 'and it is here we will be till the time of our judgment; and it is good we are and without sin' he said 'and it is good the island is where we are; for there are in it Eili and Enoch, and it is noble is the house where Eili is.' 'We would like well to see Enoch' said the clerks. 'He is in a hidden place till we all go to battle on the day of judgment' said he. And there was another thing he said to them: 'There are two lakes in this country, a lake of water and a lake of fire; and they would have gone over Ireland long ago without Martin and Patrick praying for the Gael.' Then they went on from that country and they were in the shouting of the waves for a long time till great relief came to them from God, for it is tired out they were. And they saw a great high island and everything that was in it was beautiful and holy. It is good the king was that lived in that island, and holy and just, and it is great his army was and it is noble his dwelling place was, for there were a hundred

FRIEND OF THE ANGELS OF GOD

doors in that house and an altar at every door and a dear man at every altar offering the body of Christ. And the two clerks went into the house and each of them blessed the other and after that the whole host, women and men, went to communion at the Mass. Then wine was given out to them and the king said 'Tell the men of Ireland that a great vengeance is going to fall upon them across the sea and your enemies will make war on you and will live in the half of the island. And it is what brings this vengeance upon them' he said 'the great neglect they show to the testament of God and to his teaching. And for a month and a year' he said 'you will be on the sea, but you will land safely at the last, and then let you tell out all your news to the people of Ireland.'

A HYMN COLUMCILLE MADE AND HE GOING A JOURNEY Columcille made this hymn the time the King of Teamhuir had given an order to take him, and the justice of God threw a mist about him the way he would not be known as he went out. And it is a protection to anyone that will say it, and he going on his way.

'It is alone I am on the mountain, O King-sun of the lucky road, there is nothing for me to

BOOK TWO: COLUMCILLE, THE

be in dread of. If I had threescore hundreds of armies that would defend the body, when the day of my death comes there is no strong place will hold out against it.

'He that is spent may get his death in a church or in the island in the middle of the lake; he that has luck with him, his life will be safe in the front of a battle.

'There is no one could put an end to me though he should chance upon me in danger; there is no one could protect me the day my life will come to its end.

'My life, I leave it to the will of God. There will be nothing wanting to it; there will be nothing added to it.

'He that is in health falls into sickness; he that is out of his health grows sound again; he that is in misery gets right again; he that is in good order falls into misery. Whatever God has settled for any person, he will not leave the world until he meets it; although a high head goes looking for more, he will not get the size of a grain of it.

'A man may bring a guard with him on his road; but what guard has ever kept a man from his death?

'An herb is cut for the cattle, and they after coming from the mountain. What is the

48

FRIEND OF THE ANGELS OF GOD

owner of the cattle doing that he does not cut the herb for himself?

'There is no son of a man knows for whom he is making a gathering; if it is for himself or for some other one.

'Leave out scarceness for a while; it is better for you to mind hospitality. The Son of Mary will prosper you when every guest comes to his share.

'It is often the thing that is spent comes back again, and the thing that is kept, though it is not spent it vanishes away.

'O living God! It is a pity for him that does any bad thing! The thing that is not seen comes to him; the thing that he sees goes away out of his hand.

'It is not with chance our life is; or with the bird on the top of the twig; or with the trunk of a crooked tree. It is better to put our trust in the Father, the One, and the Son.

'The share every evening in the house of God, it is what my king has made. He is the king that made the body; he will not let me go wanting to-night.

'I do not hold to the voice of birds, or any luck on the earthly world, or chance or a son or a woman. Christ the Son of God is my Druid; Christ the Son of Mary, the great

BOOK TWO : COLUMCILLE, THE
Abbot; the Father the Son and the Holy Spirit. My estates are with the King of Kings; my order is at Cenacles and Moen.'

THE LADDER OF GLASS   One time Columcille went to Monaster Boite and it is there his staff struck against the ladder of glass by which Boite had gone up to heaven; and he showed where his grave was and marked out his church. Three hundred churches he marked out & he wrote three hundred books. And among the churches he left there were a hundred that had the waves for a neighbour.

COLUMCILLE KEEPS THE FEAST OF PENTECOST   And at last one day in the month of May, Columcille went on a cart to see the brothers that were ploughing in the north of the island of Hii; and he was comforting them and teaching them. 'Well' he said 'at the Easter that went into the month of April I was ready to go to Heaven, but I had no mind you to have sorrow or trouble after your heavy work, and so I have stayed with you from Easter to Pentecost.' When his people heard those words they were very downhearted; and Columcille turned his face westward and blessed the island, and drove away from it every bad

FRIEND OF THE ANGELS OF GOD

thing. And then he came to his cell, and it was not long till there came the end of the Sabbath and the beginning of Sunday. And when he lifted his eyes he saw a great brightness, and an angel of God waiting there above him. And after that he went out, and his servant Diarmuid, whose life he had lengthened with his prayers one time he was sick, with him; and he blessed the barn and two heaps of winnowed wheat that were in it. And then he told Diarmuid he had a little secret word to tell him, that on this very night of the Sabbath of rest he would go to his own rest, on the invitation of the Lord Jesus. And he sat down on the edge of the path, for all the length of his years came upon him. And there came to him the old spent white horse that used to be carrying the milk vessels from the cowshed in the island to the brothers, and it cried tears into his breast till his clothes were wet. And Diarmuid his servant would have driven the old horse away, but Columcille said 'Leave him Diarmuid till he cries his fill, keening me. For you are a man having reason' he said 'and you know nothing of the time of my death but what I myself have told you. But as to this beast that is without reason, God

BOOK TWO: COLUMCILLE, THE

himself has made known to it in some way that its master is going to leave it. And he gave his blessing to the horse then, and it went away very sorrowful. And on the night of the Sunday of Pentecost, Columcille was the first in the church and he knelt and prayed. And the brothers came in with their candles, but the whole church was full of light, and Columcille opened his eyes wide and looked about him on every side with a great blush in his face, and they knew he was looking at the angels. And the light of the angels filled the church on every side, and he blessed the brothers, and the life went from his body, and there was a welcome before him in the household of heaven. But there are some that say he was not old when he died but young, because he had made requests of Axal the angel one time, and one of the requests was that he might die in his youth. 'For in old age' he said 'the body is ugly.' And the angel granted him that and many other things.

HOW THE NEWS WAS BROUGHT TO IRELAND   It was at the hour of his death the fishermen that were out trying for fish in the deep holes of the river Finn, saw a great light to the east that lighted up

FRIEND OF THE ANGELS OF GOD

the whole of the sky. And at Rosnaree the light of the angels was seen, and their hymns were heard in the high air. And at the same time the poets of Ireland were gathered at the yew tree at the head of Baile's Strand in Ulster, and they were making up stories there of themselves. And the things that happened did not happen the way they told them, but it was to put them on the rough race, the men of Ulster, the poets made up those lying tales. Forgaill now that was a man of Connacht and of high race, was the chief of all those poets; and news was brought to him by an angel riding a speckled horse, that Columcille was dead.

FORGAILL'S LAMENT This now is the poem of praise & of lamentation that was made for Columcille, Speckled Salmon of the Boinne, High Saint of the Gael, by Forgaill that was afterwards called Blind Forgaill, Chief Poet of Ireland:

'It is not a little story this is; it is not a story about a fool it is; it is not one district that is keening but every district, with a great sound that is not to be borne, hearing the story of Columcille, without life, without a church.

'It is not the trouble of one house, or the grief of one harpstring; all the plains

BOOK TWO: COLUMCILLE, THE

are heavy, hearing the word that is a wound.

'What way will a simple man tell of him? Even Nera from the Sidhe could not do it; he is not made much of now; our learned one is not the light of our life now he is hidden away from us.

'He that used to keep us living is dead; he that was our rightful head has died from us; he has died from us, that was God's messenger.

'The knowledgeable man that used to put fear from us is not here; the teller of words does not return to us; the teacher is gone from us that taught silence to the people.

'The whole world was his; it is a harp without its strings; it is a church without its abbot.

'Colum rose very high the time God's companies rose to meet him; it is bright the angels were, attending on him.

'It is short his life was, it is little used to satisfy him; when the wind blew the sheet against him on the sand, the shape of his ribs could be seen through it.

'He was the head of every gathering; he was a dun of the book of the law; he put a flame in the district of the north, he lightened the district of the west; the east was his

FRIEND OF THE ANGELS OF GOD

along with it; he did not open his heart to every company. Good his death; he went with God's angels that came to meet him.

'He has reached to Axal of his help and to the troops of the archangels; he has reached to a place where night is not seen; he has reached to a plain where music has not to be born; where no one listens to oppression. The King of priests has done away with his troubles.

'He knew the way he was going; he gave kindness for hatred; he learned psalms; he broke the battle against hunger.

'He knew seasons and storms; he read the secrets of the great wisdom; he knew the course of the moon; he took notice of its race with the branching sun. He was skilful in the course of the sea; to tell every high thing we have heard from Colum, would be to count the stars of heaven.

'A healer of the heart of the wise; a full satisfier of guests; our crowned one who spoke with Axal; a shelter to the naked; a comforter to the poor; he was eager, he was noble, it is high his death was. We hope great honour will be given to him on the head of these deeds.'

And when Forgaill had made that lament he

BOOK TWO: COLUMCILLE, THE

said: 'It is a great shaping and a great finish I have given to these words, and I cannot make a praise beyond this, for my eyes have been taken from me.'

It was Aedh King of Ireland gave seven cumhals for his name to be given in the praising of Columcille; and Aedh laid it down to Forgaill that this song should be above every other song. But it was after death the reward and the praise were given to blind Forgaill; for it was Heaven that was given to him, as the price of the praising of the King.

COLUMCILLE'S BURYING PLACE   It is an old saying in Ireland that if Columcille died in Hii, his soul is in Doire and his body under a flagstone in Ardmacha beside Brigit and Patrick. But one time when some person that was looking at the church in Hii told that saying, the people of the island were very angry, and said the Irish were impudent liars to say such a thing, and that Saint Columcille had been buried in their island, and none had ever come to bring him away, and if they had they would not have got him. But it is what the people of Ireland say to this day, that when he was dying he bade the brothers to put his body in a currach and to cut directions on a stick and to put the currach

FRIEND OF THE ANGELS OF GOD

out to sea. So they did that and the currach floated to the north of Ireland, but not one knew of it being there. And there were a few cows that had pasture near the sea, and one of them used to be going down to the shore every day, and to be licking a brown stick that was lying there. And the boy that was minding them took notice that the milk that cow gave was three times more than the milk of every other cow, and he wondered to see the cow that was the scarcest of all giving milk and butter like that, and it eating nothing, but only licking a bit of a stick. So they went and looked at the stick, and they read on it that Saint Columcille's body was in the currach and they found it there; but whether it was only his bones they found, or whether he was embalmed, being such a great man, is not known. And the writing on the stick said he was to be buried in Ardmacha, between Saint Patrick and Saint Brigit. And they did not know where those graves were, but they brought the body to Ardmacha, and the ground opened of itself, and they knew it was to let him rest between those two it opened.

COLUMCILLE'S VALLEY   Bran, now, the hound of Finn son of Cumhail, stopped one time at the hunting, and

BOOK TWO

would not follow a deer through a certain valley. And it was always said, she knew that to be a valley Columcille would bless in the time to come. And the people of Slieve Echtge say there will be a great war yet in the whole world and in Ireland, and the want will be so great that the father will disown his son and will not let him in at the door. And there will be great fighting on Slieve-nan-Or, the Golden Mountain, and in the Valley of the Black Pig. And when the war comes as far as the blessed bush at Kilchriest, a priest will put on his stole, and will read from his book, and lift a chalice three times, and that will weaken it for a while. But the fighting will never reach to the Valley of Columcille; and it will be well for all the people that will be in that valley at the time of the last great war.

BOOK THREE:
BLESSED PATRICK OF THE BELLS

THE FOUR HOUSEHOLDS There were many great saints among the Gael, but Patrick was the bush among them all. It was beyond the sea he was born, and his mother was a sister of Saint Martin of Tours; and he dreamed in Rome, and walked all Ireland barefoot. It was in his young youth he was brought from France to Ireland as a slave, and he was set to serve four households, and he did his work so well that every one of the households thought him to be servant to itself alone; and it was by an angel the ashes used to be cleared away from the hearth for him.

HE GETS HIS FREEDOM He was sent out after a while minding swine & he went through great hardships; but Victor the angel used to come to visit him and to teach him the order of prayer. And he had no way to buy his freedom, but one time a wild boar came rooting in the field, and brought up a lump of gold; and Patrick brought it to a tinker and the tinker said 'It is nothing but solder, give it here to me.' But then he brought it to a smith, and the smith told him it was gold, and with that gold he bought his freedom. And from that time the smiths

BOOK THREE: BLESSED

have been lucky, taking money every day and never without work; but as for the tinkers, every man's face is against them and their face is against every man, and they get no ease or rest, but are ever and always travelling the world.

THE MAN AND WO-MAN THAT WERE ALWAYS YOUNG

After that he went out to sea with foreigners and he went back to his own country, and his people asked him to stop there with them. But he would not; for always in his sleep he could see the island of the Gael, and he could hear the singing of the children of the Wood of Fochlad. He went over the sea of Icht then, and he fasted in the islands of the Torrian sea, and then he went to learn from Germanus, and after that again to Rome. And then he and his people went out to sea, nine in all, and they came to an island where they saw a new house, and a young man and a young woman in it; and they saw a withered old hag by the door of the house. 'What happened this old woman?' said Patrick. 'It is great her weakness is.' 'She is my own grandchild, old as she is,' said the young man. 'What way did that happen?' said Patrick. 'It is not hard to say that' said

PATRICK OF THE BELLS

the young man; 'For we are here from the time of Christ' he said 'and he came to visit us when he was here among men, and we made a feast for him and he blessed our house and he blessed ourselves, but the blessing did not reach to our children. And this is the way we will be, without age coming upon us, to the Judgement. And it is a long time your coming is foretold to us' he said 'and it is the will of God for you to go and to preach in the country of the Gael; and Christ left a token with us, a bent staff to be given to you.'

PATRICK GOES BACK TO IRELAND Patrick took the staff with him then & went back to Germanus. And Victor the angel came and said to him 'It was God's bidding to you to go back and to teach in the country of the Gael.' But Patrick was not willing to go and he complained to God of the hardheartedness of the Gael. And God said 'I myself will be your helper.' Then Patrick went back to Rome and he was made a bishop, and when they were making a bishop of him the three quires answered to them, the quire of the people of Heaven, the quire of the Romans and the quire of the children of the Wood of Fochlad. It was in

BOOK THREE: BLESSED

the east of Ireland he landed, at Inis Patrick; and three times before that the druids had foretold his coming, and it is what they said, 'Adzeheads will come over an angry sea; their cloaks hole-headed; their staves crooked; their tables to the east of their houses; they will all answer Amen.' At the time he landed it was the feast of Beltaine, and on that day every year the High King lighted a fire in Teamhuir, and there was geasa, that is a bond, upon the men of Ireland not to kindle a fire in any place before the kindling of that fire in Teamhuir. Patrick, now, struck the flame of the Paschal fire, and all the people saw it and it lighted up the whole of Magh Breg. 'That is a breaking of bonds' said the king to his druids; 'and find out for me' he said 'who was it kindled that fire.' And it is what the druids said, 'Unless that fire is quenched before morning in the same night it was kindled, it will never be quenched.' And when the fire was not quenched in that night, there was great anger on the king.

THE DEER'S CRY Patrick made this hymn one time he was going to preach the Faith at Teamhuir, and his enemies lay in hiding to make an attack on him as he passed. But

PATRICK OF THE BELLS

as he himself and Benen his servant went by, all they could see passing was a wild deer and a fawn. And the Deer's Cry is the name of the hymn to this day.

'I bind myself to-day to a strong strength, to a calling on the Trinity. I believe in a Threeness with confession of a Oneness in the Creator of the World.

'I bind myself to-day to the strength of Christ's birth and his baptism; to the strength of his crucifixion with his burial; to the strength of his resurrection with his ascension;

'In stability of earth, in steadfastness of rock, I bind to myself to-day God's strength to pilot me;

'God's power to uphold me; God's wisdom to guide me; God's eye to look before me; God's ear to hear me;

'God's word to speak for me; God's hand to guard me; God's path to lie before me; God's shield to protect me; God's host to save me;

'Against snares of demons; against the begging of sins; against the asking of nature; against all my ill-wishers near me and far from me; alone and in a crowd.

'So I have called on all these strengths, to

BOOK THREE: BLESSED

come between me and every fierce and merciless strength that may come between my body and my soul;

'Against incantations of false prophets; against black laws of heathens; against false laws of heretics; against craft of idolatry; against spells of women and smiths and druids; against every knowledge forbidden to the souls of men;

'Christ for my protection to-day against poison, against burning, against drowning, against wounding; that a multitude of rewards may come to me.

'Christ with me, Christ before me; Christ behind me, Christ in me; Christ under me, Christ over me; Christ to the right of me, Christ to the left of me; Christ in lying down, Christ in sitting, Christ in rising up;

'Christ in the heart of everyone that thinks of me; Christ in the mouth of everyone that speaks to me; Christ in every eye that sees me; Christ in every ear that hears me.

'I bind to myself to-day a strong strength to a calling upon the Trinity; I believe in a Threeness with confession of a Oneness in the Creator of the World!'

PATRICK AND THE BIG MEN It is often told by the people of Ireland how

PATRICK OF THE BELLS

Oisin, son of Finn, came back to Ireland in the time of Patrick; and the poets of Ireland have put into verses the arguments they used to be having with one another. And there are some say Caoilte of the Fianna and a troop of his people were in Ireland at that same time; and whether or not that story is true, this is the way the meeting between himself and Patrick is put down in the old writings.

Patrick was one time singing the Mass at the Rath of the Red Ridge where Finn, son of Cumhal, used to be, and his clerks were with him. And the clerks saw Caoilte and his people coming towards them, and fear and terror fell on them before the great men and the great hounds that were with them; for they were not of the one time with themselves. It is then there rose up that high herdsman, that angel of the earth, Patrick son of Calpurn, Apostle of the Gael, and sprinkled holy water upon the big men, and with that every bad thing that was about them made away into the hills and the scalps and the borders of the country on every side, and the big men sat down. And there was great wonder on the clerks as they looked at them, for the tallest of themselves reached

BOOK THREE: BLESSED

but to their waist or to their shoulders, and they sitting. 'What name have you?' said Patrick then. 'I am Caoilte, son of Ronan of the Fianna.' 'Was it not a good lord you were with' said Patrick 'that is Finn, son of Cumhal?' And Caoilte said 'If the brown leaves falling in the woods were gold, if the waves of the sea were silver, Finn would have given away the whole of it.' 'What was it kept you through your lifetime?' said Patrick. 'Truth that was in our hearts, and strength in our hands, and fulfilment in our tongues' said Caoilte. Then Patrick gave them food and drink and good treatment and talked with them. And on the morning of the morrow his two protecting angels came to him out on the green, and he asked them was it any harm before the King of Heaven and earth, for him to be listening to the stories of the Fianna. And it is what the angels answered him: 'Holy Clerk' they said 'it is no more than a third of their stories these old fighting-men can tell, by reason of forgetfulness and their memory that fails them; but whatever they tell, let you write it down on poet's boards and in the words of poets, for it will be a diversion to the companies and the high people of the latter times

PATRICK OF THE BELLS

to be listening to them.' And Patrick did as they bade him, and he bade Brogan the scribe to write down all the stories told by Caoilte; and Brogan did that, and they are in the world to this day.

THE HIDDEN WELL OF USNACH   One time Diarmuid king of Ireland was with Patrick on the Hill of Usnach, and there was no water to be had; and one of the big men of the Fianna, it might have been Caoilte and it might have been Oisin, asked for a vessel that he might go and get it. And as he went he was looking back to see were they watching him, and when he was out of their sight he went to the Well of Usnach that was called the Whitebrimmed, and since the time of the battle of Gabra it had never been found by any man in Ireland. And when he came to the brink of the well he saw in it eight beautiful speckled salmon, for it was such a hidden place there was nothing for them to be in dread of. He took then eight sprigs of watercress and eight of brooklime, and he put down the vessel into the well and he took the eight salmon alive and leaping like mad things. And then he went back and set the vessel before the King of Ireland, and there was wonder on

BOOK THREE: BLESSED

them all seeing that; and the stalk of every one of the sprigs of the watercress reached as high as Diarmuid's knee. 'They must be divided into two shares' he said 'a half to Patrick and a half to ourselves.' 'Not so' said Patrick 'for there are more of you than of ourselves. But make three parts' he said 'and give one to the church for that is her own share;' and so it was done. 'That is well, King of Ireland' he said then 'but do not lose your share in heaven through these big men.' 'What do you mean saying that?' said Diarmuid. 'I mean that you have your thoughts too much taken up with them' said Patrick.

PATRICK AND CASCORACH THE MUSICIAN One time the King of Ulster went up with Caoilte to a great liss that was called Foradh-na-Feinne, the Resting-place of the Fianna. And when they were there they saw coming towards them a young man that was wearing a beautiful green cloak having in it a silver brooch; a shirt of yellow silk next his skin he had; a coat of soft satin, and a harp from his neck. 'Where do you come from and who are you yourself?' said the King. 'I come from the South from the Hill of Bodb Dearg son of the Dagda,' said he; 'and I am Cascorach, son of Cainchen

PATRICK OF THE BELLS

that is poet to the Tuatha de Danaan and I am the makings of a poet myself. And it is what I am come for now' he said 'to get true knowledge and the stories of the Fianna and their great deeds from Caoilte son of Ronan.' With that he took his harp and made music for them till he had put them all into their sleep. 'Well Caoilte my soul' he said then 'what answer will you give me?' 'I will give you all you are asking' said Caoilte 'if you have skill and understanding to learn all the Fianna did of arms and of bravery. And it was a great fighting-man used to be in this place' he said 'that was Finn, son of Cumhal, 'and it is great riches and great wages you would have got from him for your music; although this day the place is empty.' And he made this lament:

'The Resting-place of the Fianna is bare to-night where Finn of the naked sword used to be; through the death of the king that was without gloom, wide Almhuin is deserted;

'The high company are not living; Finn the very prince is not alive; no armies to be seen, no captains with the King of the Fianna.

'They are all gone, the people of Finn, they that used to be going from valley to valley; it is a pity the life I have now, to be left after

BOOK THREE: BLESSED

Diarmuid and Conan, after Goll son of Morna from the plain.
'It is the truth I am telling you; all that I say is true; it is great our losses were there beyond. They are gone, the armies and the hundreds; it is a pity I myself not to have found death; they are all gone now; they used to be together from border to border.'
Then Caoilte brought to mind the loss of the heroes and of the great companies he used to be going among, and he cried miserably, sorrowfully, till all his breast was wet with him. He set out after that and Cascorach with him and they went up by hills and rocks to the top of green-grassed Slieve Fuad, to the rowan tree of the Meadow of the Two Stags and to the place where the men of Ulster left their chariots after the last battle of the War for the Bull of Cuailgne. And Patrick was there before him, having with him three times fifty bishops and three times fifty priests and three times fifty deacons and three times fifty singers of psalms. And they sat down there, and Patrick kept his Hours with praising the Maker of the world. Then he gave a welcome to Caoilte. 'Well, my soul' he said 'who is that well-looking dark-eyebrowed curly-headed young man that is with

PATRICK OF THE BELLS

you, having a harp with him?' 'He is Cascorach son of the musician of the Tuatha De Danaan, that is come to find news and knowledge of the Fianna from me.' 'It is a good road he has chosen' said Patrick. 'And O Caoilte' he said 'it is great good you yourself have waited for, the time of belief and of saints and of holiness, and to be in friendship with the King of Heaven and earth. And play to us now Cascorach' he said 'till we hear your music and your skill.' 'I will do that' said Cascorach; 'and I never was better pleased, holy Clerk, to do it for any man than for yourself.' He took his harp then and readied it, and played a strain of music, and the clerks had never heard the like of that music for sweetness, unless it might be the praises of the King of Heaven sung according to the Rule. And they all fell into their sleep listening to the continuous music of the Sidhe. And when Cascorach had made an end of playing, he asked a reward of Patrick. 'What reward are you asking, my soul?' said Patrick. 'Heaven for myself' said he 'for that is the reward is best; and good luck to go with my art and with all that will follow it after me.' 'I give you heaven' said Patrick, 'and I give this to your art, it to be one of

BOOK THREE: BLESSED

the three arts by which a man can find profit to the last in Ireland. And however great the grudgingness a man of your art may meet with, let him but make his music, and no one will begrudge him anything. 'And that they may have all happiness' he said, 'so long as they are not slothful in their trade.' After that Cascorach put back his harp in its covering. 'That was good music you gave us' said Brogan the scribe. 'It was good indeed' said Patrick; 'and but for a taste of the music of the Sidhe that was in it I never heard anything nearer to the music of heaven.' 'If there is music in heaven why should it not be on earth?' said Brogan. 'And so it is not right to banish it away.' 'I do not say we should banish it' said Patrick, 'but only that we should not hold to it out of measure.'

PATRICK'S FAREWELL TO CAOILTE But after a good while Caoilte said 'Holy Patrick, my soul, I am thinking it is time for me to be going to-morrow.' 'Why would you go?' said Patrick. 'To be searching out the hills and the hollows of every place where my comrades and the King of the Fianna used to be together with me, for it seems long to me to be in the one place.' And

PATRICK OF THE BELLS

when they rose up on the morrow, Caoilte laid his hand in Patrick's bosom and it is what Patrick said 'From myself to yourself, in the house or out of the house, in whatever place God will lay his hand on you, I give you Heaven.'

BODB DEARG'S DAUGHTER Aedh King of Connacht was at Dun Leoda Loingsig one time giving a great feast. And it happened at the fall of the clouds of evening he came out on the green lawn, and as he was there and the people of his household with him, he saw on one side a girl of wonderful appearance, having yellow hair, and she not looking at the people but only at the king. 'Where do you come from girl?' said the king. 'Out of the shining Brugh in the east' said she. 'For what cause are you come?' said the king. 'You are my sweetheart,' said she. 'Whose daughter are you and what name have you?' said the king. 'I am Aillenn of the many shapes, daughter to Bodb Dearg, son of the Dagda. 'I have never seen a woman I would sooner have as a wife than yourself' said the king 'but that I am under the rule of Blessed Patrick and of the King of Heaven and earth. And Patrick bound me' he said 'to have one wife only, that is Aife daughter of Eoghan,

BOOK THREE: BLESSED

King of Leinster. And would you wish to be seen by the great men of my kingdom?' he said. 'I would like it indeed' said she 'for I am not an everliving woman of the Sidhe, but I am of the Tuatha de Danaan, having my own body about me.' Then she showed herself to the whole gathering of the people and they never saw before or after a woman more beautiful than herself. 'And what judgment do you put upon me King?' she said. 'Whatever judgment Blessed Patrick gives I will give it' said he. Then Aedh sent messengers to Patrick where he was in the south, and they brought him to Beinn Gulbain in Maenmag. And Aedh the King went to meet him there and knelt before him and told him the whole story. 'Are you the girl' said Patrick 'that gave her love to the King of Connacht?' 'I am' said she. 'Well girl' said Patrick 'it is good your shape is and your appearance. And what is it keeps you like this' he said 'at the very height of your comeliness?' 'Everyone that drank at Giobniu's Feast' she said, 'no sickness or wasting comes upon them. And tell me now holy Clerk' she said 'what is your judgment on myself and on the King of Connacht?' 'It is a good one' said Patrick; 'it is settled by God and myself

PATRICK OF THE BELLS

that a man must have one wife only.' 'And I myself' said the girl 'what am I to do?' 'Go back to your house among the Sidhe' said Patrick; 'and if it should happen the King of Leinster's daughter to die before yourself, let the man you have given your love to take you as his only wife. But if you should try to harm Aedh or his wife by day or by night' he said 'I will destroy you the way neither your father or your mother or your fosterers will like to be looking at you.' Then the girl cried pitifully, heavily, and the King said 'I am dear to you.' 'You are dear to me indeed' said she. 'There is not one of the people of the world is dearer to me than yourself' said the king; 'but I must not go beyond the conditions of the Adzehead and of God.' With that the girl went back to her hidden house among the Sidhe. And after a while the wife of the King of Connacht died at Uaran Garaid and was buried on the hill that is called the High Place of the Angels. And after that again there was a gathering made of all the five provinces of Ireland to hold the feast of Teamhuir. And Patrick and Aedh King of Connacht were out on the green; and they saw coming towards them Aillenn daughter of Bodb Dearg, having with her three fifties of

BOOK THREE: BLESSED

the women of the Tuatha de Danaan, and she sat down on the grass beside Patrick and the King of Connacht, and she gave her message. Then Patrick said to the King 'I will give her to you if you will take her as your wife.' 'Whatever you are willing for me to do I will do it' said the King. 'I promised you would take her' said Patrick, 'if she would give up her false druid belief and kneel to the King of heaven and earth.' 'Do you agree to that Aillenn?' said the king. 'I agree to it' said she. Then she rose up, and her women, and they all kneeled to Patrick, and Patrick joined her and the King in marriage. That now was the first marriage made by the Adzehead in Ireland.

ETHNE THE BEAUTIFUL AND FEDELM THE ROSY-RED

Patrick was one time at Cruachan of Connacht, and he went up to the well that is called Clibach and that is opposite the rising of the sun, and he sat down beside the well, and his clerks with him. There were two daughters now of Laoghaire the High King were living at Rath Cruachan at that time, getting their learning from the druids, and the name of the one was Ethne and the other was Fedelm the Rosy-Red. And it was their custom every morning to come and to wash them-

PATRICK OF THE BELLS

selves in the well. And on this day when they came they saw a company of men having white clothes, and books before them beside the well. And there was great wonder on them and they thought them to be of the people of the Sidhe. And they questioned Patrick and said to him 'Where do you come from? And where are you going? And is it gods you are' they said 'or men from the hills of the Sidhe?' 'It would be better for you to believe in God than to be asking who we ourselves are' said Patrick. 'Who is your God?' said Ethne then. 'And where is he?' she said 'Is it in the skies he is, or in the earth, or under the earth, or upon the earth, or in the seas or in the streams, or in the mountains or in the valleys? And has he riches?' she said 'Is he young? Is he beautiful? Has he sons and daughters? Is he of the everliving ones?' Patrick took in hand then to answer their questions and to teach them the true faith; and he told them it was fitting they should join with the King of Glory, being as they were the daughters of an earthly king. And when they had heard the whole story a great desire came upon them to serve Him. 'And it is the desire of our hearts' they said 'to see his Son, our husband.' 'That is

BOOK THREE: BLESSED

not possible' said Patrick 'but through taking the body of Christ and through death.' 'We would die surely' they said 'if we might see Christ on the moment.' Then Patrick baptized them and gave them the Body of Christ, and put a white veil upon their heads, and they were filled with peace and with the friendship of God. And when they were sleeping in death, his people put them on a little bed and laid coverings over them, and keened them there.

THE SOUL AND THE BODY   The Saviour told Patrick one time to go and prepare a man that was going to die. And Patrick said 'I would sooner not go for I never yet saw the soul part from the body.' But after that he went and prepared the man. And when he was lying there dead, he saw the soul go from the body, and three times it went to the door and three times it came back and kissed the body. And Patrick asked the Saviour why it did that and he said 'That soul was sorry to part from the body because it had kept it so clean and so honest.'

PATRICK'S RUSH CANDLES   Patrick went one time into a house in the south, and the people of it were poor, and they had not a candle or a rushlight or turf or sticks

PATRICK OF THE BELLS

for a fire, but when the daylight was done what they had to do was to go to their bed. And when Patrick came in and saw the house so dark he said 'Are there no green rushes growing in the bog?' So they went out and brought him in a bundle of green rushes and he took them in his hand and blessed them, and they gave out light through the whole of the night time.

HIS CHURCH AT ARDMACHA   Patrick was walking up the hill of Ardmacha one time with his people and they found a doe resting on the ground, and a fawn beside her. And his people were going to kill the fawn, but Patrick forbade them and he took it in his arms and carried it, and the doe came following after him. And it was in the place where he put down the fawn, the church of Ardmacha was built for him afterwards.

HE IS WAKED BY THE ANGELS   When the time came for Patrick to die it is to Ardmacha he had a desire to go. But Victor the angel went to meet him on the road at midday and said 'Go back to the place you came from, to the barn, for it is there your death will be. And give thanks to Christ' he said 'for your prayers are granted;

BOOK THREE

it is to Heaven you will soon be going.' And when his soul parted from his body, there was no candle wasted with him, but it was the angels of God kept lasting watch over him until the end of twelve nights, and through all that time there was no night in Magh Inis with the light of the angels. It is that was a long day of peace! And after his death there was near being a great battle between the men of Ulster and the Ua Neill, fighting for his body. But at the last it seemed to them that his body was brought by each of them to his own country, and so they were separated by God.

BOOK FOUR:
THE VOYAGE OF MAELDUNE THE QUEEN'S FOSTER-SON

There was a great man of the Eoganacht of the Arans, Ailill of the Edge of Battle his name was. And one time he went with the king making war he fell in with a woman of Kildare, and he forced her; and she bade him to tell her his race and his name. And it was not long after that, he was killed by robbers in his own place, and they burned his church over him. And at the end of nine months the woman gave birth to a son, and she gave him the name of Maeldune. And after a while she brought him in secret to the Queen, that was her friend, and it was by the Queen Maeldune was reared, and she gave out that she was his mother; and the one fostermother reared him and the King's three sons in the one cradle and on the one breast and the one knee. It is beautiful indeed Maeldune was, and it is likely there was never anyone so beautiful as himself, and he grew up to be a young man, fit to use weapons, and it is quiet he was and pleasant in his ways. And in his play he went beyond all his comrades, in throwing of balls and in running and leaping, and in racing of horses, for it is he took the sway in all these things. One day now a proud fighting man

BOOK FOUR : THE

got to be jealous of him and he said in the dint of his anger 'You' he said 'whose race and kindred no one knows, and whose father and mother no one knows, to be getting the better of us in every game, whether by land or by water or on the draughtboard.' Maeldune was silent when he heard that, for till that time he thought himself to be a son of the king and of the queen his fostermother. And he went to her and said to her 'I will not eat and I will not drink' he said 'till you tell me of my mother and my father.' 'Why are you asking after that?' said she. 'Do not give heed to the words of the young men. It is I am your mother' she said 'and the love of no person on earth for a son is greater than my love for you.' 'That may be so' he said 'but for all that, it is right for you to make known my own parents to me.'

So his fostermother went with him, and gave him into the hand of his mother, and on that he asked his mother to tell him who was his father. 'It is foolishness to ask that' she said 'for if you should know your father itself it would not serve you, and you would be no better off for it is long ago he died.' 'It is better for me to know it' said he 'however it may be.' His mother told him the truth then.

VOYAGE OF MAELDUNE

'Ailill of the Edge of Battle was your father' she said 'of the Eoganacht of Aran.' Then Maeldune went to his father's place and to his own inheritance, and his three fosterbrothers with him, and it is kind champions they were. And his kindred welcomed them, and they bade him keep good courage. It was some time after that, the graveyard of the Church of Duncluain was full of fighting men that were casting stones; and Maeldune's foot was on the burned wall of the church, and he casting the stone over it. And a bitter-tongued man of the people of the church said to Maeldune, 'It would be better' he said 'you to avenge the man that was burned there than to be casting stones over his bare burned bones.' 'What man was that?' said Maeldune. 'It was Ailill' he said 'your own father.' 'Who was it killed him?' said Maeldune. 'It was outlaws of Laighis' he said 'and it was here on this spot he was destroyed.' Then Maeldune threw the stone from him, and took his cloak around him and his fighting-dress, and he was sorrowful doing it. And he asked what way could he go to Laighis, and those that knew it said he could not go there but by sea only. So he went into the country of Corcomruadh

BOOK FOUR: THE

to ask a charm and good luck of a druid that was there, till he would begin building a boat. The druid told Maeldune what day he should begin his boat, and the number that should go in it, seventeen men, no more and no less; and he told him the day he should set out to sea. Then Maeldune made a boat having three skins on it, and those that were to go with him made ready; German was of them, and Diuran the half-poet. He set out on the sea the same day the druid had bade him, and when they were gone a little from the land after hoisting the sail, there came to the harbour his three fosterbrothers, and they called to him to let them go with him. 'Go back home' said Maeldune 'for if I was to go back itself I would not bring with me but the number that is here.' 'We will go into the sea after you and be drowned if you will not come back to us' they said. Then the three of them threw themselves into the sea and swam out from the land; and when Maeldune saw that, he turned back to them that they might not be drowned, and brought them into the currach to him.

THE LITTLE BALD ISLANDS They were rowing that day till vespers, and the

VOYAGE OF MAELDUNE

night after till midnight, till they found two little bald islands having two duns in them; and they heard coming out from the duns the cries and the outcry of drunkenness and of the soldiers with their spoils. And it is what they heard one man saying to another 'Keep off from me' he said 'for I am a better champion than yourself, for it is I killed Ailill of the Edge of Battle, and burned Duncluain on him, and his kindred have done nothing against me; and you never did the like of that' he said. 'We have the victory in our hands' said German and Diuran the half-poet. 'It is God brought us here and that directed our boat. And let us go and make an attack on those duns' he said 'since God has showed us our enemies.' While they were saying those words a great wind came upon them, the way they were driven all that night until morning. And even after daybreak they did not see land or earth, and they did not know where they were going. Then Maeldune said 'Leave the boat quiet without rowing, and wherever God has a mind to bring it, let it go.' Then they came into the great ocean that has no ending, and it is what Maeldune said to his fosterbrothers. 'It is you have done that on us, throwing yourselves upon us in the boat against the word of the druid that told us not to let come in the boat but the number we were before you came.' And they had no answer to give, only to stay in their silence for a while.

THE ISLAND OF ANTS Three days and three nights they were, and they did not find land nor ground. And on the morning of the third day they heard a sound from the north-east. 'That is the sound of a wave against the shore' said German. And when the day was light, they went towards land, and as they were casting lots to know who should go on shore, there came a great swarm of ants, every one of them the size of a foal, down to the strand towards them and into the sea, as if to devour them and their boat. So Maeldune and his men made away and were going over the sea for three days and three nights, and they saw neither land nor ground.

THE ISLAND OF BIRDS The morning of the third day they heard the sound of waves against the strand, and they saw with the light of day an island, big and high, and ridges about it, every one of them lower than the other, and trees around it, and great birds on the trees. And they were consult-

VOYAGE OF MAELDUNE

ing together who would go and search the island, and see what kind were the birds. 'I will go' said Maeldune. So he went and he searched the island, and he found no harmful thing in it, and they ate their fill of the birds and brought more of them into the boat.

THE BEAST THAT WAS LIKE A HORSE Three days and three nights they were on the sea after that, but on the morning of the fourth day they saw another great island having sandy soil. And when they came to the shore they saw a beast on it that was like a horse. Legs of a hound he had with rough sharp nails, and it is a great welcome he gave them, and he was moving about before them; for he was covetous to devour themselves and their boat. 'It is not sorry he is to meet with us' said Maeldune; 'and let us go out from the island.' They did that, and when the beast saw them going from him, he went down to the strand, and he was digging it up with his sharp nails and pelting them, that they did not think to escape from him.

THE DEMON RIDERS They rowed a long way after that, till they saw a great level island before them. And it was

BOOK FOUR: THE

on German there fell a bad lot to go and to search that island. 'The both of us will go' said Diuran the half-poet; 'and you will come with me another time when I am to search out an island.' So the two of them went into the island, and it is great its size was, and its length, and they saw in it a long green lawn, having hoof marks of horses on it, and every hoof mark was the size of the sail of a ship. And along with that they saw the shells of very large nuts and they saw what was like the leavings of food of many people, and they were in dread of what they saw, and they called to the rest of their people to come and see what they saw. There was fear on them all after that, and they made no delay and went back into their boat. And when they had gone out a little from the land they saw rushing over the sea to the island a great troop, that when they reached to the green on the island began racing their horses. And it is quicker than the wind every horse was, and it is great was the noise and the shouting. And Maeldune could hear the strokes of the rods on the horses, and he could hear what everyone of them was saying: 'Bring the grey horse' 'Drive the brown horse there beyond' 'Bring the white one'

VOYAGE OF MAELDUNE

'My horse is the quickest' 'Mine is the best at the leaps!' And when they heard those words they made away with all their might, for they were sure it was a gathering of demons they were looking at.

A HOUSE OF PLENTY   Then they were going on through the length of a week in hunger and in thirst till they found an island very big and high, and a large house at the edge of the sea, and a door in the house towards the level plain of the island, and another door towards the sea, and against that door there was a weir of stone, and an opening in it, and the waves of the sea were throwing salmon through the opening into the middle of the house. The wanderers went into the house then, and they found no one in it, but what they saw was a very large bed for the head man of the house only, and a bed for every three of his people, and food for three before every bed, and a glass vessel with good drink in it before every bed, and a cup for every vessel. So they made a meal off that food and that drink, and they gave thanks to Almighty God that had given them relief from their hunger.

THE APPLE ROD   When they went from that island they were going for a

BOOK FOUR: THE

long time hungry and without food, till they found another island, and a high cliff around it on every side, and a long narrow wood in it, very long and very narrow. When Maeldune reached to that wood he took a rod in his hand, and he passing by. Three days and three nights the rod was in his hand, and the currach under sail going along by the cliff. And on the third day he found a cluster of three apples at the end of the rod. And through forty nights they were satisfied with those apples.

THE WHIRLING BEAST They came then to another island, and a wall of stone around it. And when they came near, a great beast leaped up and went racing about the island, and it seemed to Maeldune to be going quicker than the wind. And it went then to the high part of the island, and it did the straightening-of-the-body feat, that is, its head below and its feet above; and it is the way it used to be, it turned in its skin, the flesh and the bones going around but the skin outside without moving. And at another time the skin outside would turn like a mill, and the flesh and the bones not stirring. That now is the way it was, and it going around the island. Maeldune and his people

VOYAGE OF MAELDUNE

made away then with all their might, and the beast saw them running, and it made for the strand to get hold of them and it began to strike at them, and it was casting stones at them, and one of the stones came into the currach and it broke through Maeldune's shield, and lodged in the keel of the currach.

THE WICKED HORSES   It was not long after that they found another high island, and it is delightful it was, and there were great beasts in it like horses. Everyone of them would take a piece out of the side of another and bring it away with its skin and its flesh, the way there were streams of red blood breaking out of their sides till the ground was full of it. So they left that island in haste and as if out of their wits, and they did not know where in the world were they going, or in what place they would find help or land or country.

THE FIERY PIGS   Then they came to another island, and they worn out with hunger and thirst, sad and tired without hope of relief. And in that island there were a great many fruit trees, having large golden apples upon them. And there were beasts like pigs, short and fiery, under those trees, and they used to go to the trees and to

BOOK FOUR: THE

strike them with their hind legs till the apples would fall from them, and then they would feed on them. And from morning to the setting of the sun those beasts did not show themselves at all, but they used to be stopping in caves of the ground. And round about that island there were a great many birds out on the waves; from matins to nones they used to be swimming away from the island, but from nones to vespers they used to come back towards the island and they would reach to it at the going down of the sun; and then they used to be stripping off the apples and to be eating them. 'Let us go into the island where those birds are' said Maeldune, 'for it is not harder for us to go there than for the birds.' One of his men went to search the island then, and he called his comrade to him. It is hot the ground was under their feet, and they could not stop there because of the heat, for it was a fiery country, and the beasts used to throw out heat into the ground that was over them. They brought away a few of the apples with them that first day to be eating in the currach. And with the brightness of the morning the birds went from the island, swimming out to sea; and with that the fiery beasts began putting up their heads out

VOYAGE OF MAELDUNE

of the caves, and they were eating the apples until the setting of the sun. And when they would go back into the caves, the birds used to come and to be eating the apples. And Maeldune went and his people and they gathered up all the apples that were in it that night. And those apples drove away both hunger and thirst from them, and they filled their boat with them, and put out again to sea.

THE LITTLE CAT   And when those apples failed them, and their hunger was great and their thirst, and when their mouths and their nostrils were full of the salt of the sea, they got sight of an island that was no great size, having a dun in it, and a high wall around the dun, as white as if it was built of burned lime, or as if it was all one rock of chalk, and it is great its height was from the sea and it all to reached to the clouds. The dun was wide open, and there were many new white houses around it. And when Maeldune and his men went into the best of the houses they saw no one in it but a little cat that was in the middle of the house, and it playing about on the four stone pillars that were there, and leaping from one to another. It looked at the men for a short

BOOK FOUR: THE

space, but it did not stop from its play. After that they saw three rows on the wall of the house round about, from one doorpost to another; the first was a row of brooches of gold and silver, and their pins in the wall, and the second was a row of collars of gold and of silver, every one of them like the hoops of a vat; and the third row was of great swords having hilts of gold and of silver. And the rooms were full of white coverings and of shining clothes, and there was a roasted ox and a fire in the middle of the house, and large vessels with good fermented drink. 'Is it for us this is left here?' said Maeldune to the cat. It looked at him for a minute and took to its playing again, and Maeldune knew then it was for them the feast had been left. So they eat and they drank and they slept, and they stored up what was left of the food and of the drink. And when they thought of going, Maeldune's third fosterbrother said to him 'Might I bring away with me a necklace of these necklaces?' 'Do not' said Maeldune, 'for it is not without a guard this house is.' But in spite of that he brought it with him as far as the middle of the dun. And the cat came after him and leaped through him like a fiery arrow and burned him till he was

VOYAGE OF MAELDUNE

but ashes, and it made a leap back again to its pillar. Maeldune quieted the cat then with his words, and he put back the necklace in its place, and cleared away the ashes from the floor, and threw them on the shore of the sea. And then they went back into the currach, praising and making much of the Lord.

THE WAR OF COLOURS Early on the morning of the third day after that, they saw another island having a wall of brass over the middle of it, that divided it in two parts; and they saw great flocks of sheep in it, a black flock on the near side of the fence and a white flock on the far side, and they saw a big man separating the flocks. When he used to throw a white sheep over the near side of the fence to the black sheep, it would turn to black on the moment; and when he used to throw a black sheep over the fence to the far side, it would turn to white in the same way. There was dread on the men when they saw that. 'It is best for us' said Maeldune 'to throw two rods into the island, and if they change their colour we will know that our own colour would change.' So they threw a rod having black bark on the side where the white sheep were, and it turned to white there and then. Then they threw a peeled white rod on the side where the black sheep were, and it turned to black. 'That is no good sign' said Maeldune; 'and let us not land on the island. It is likely our own colour would have lasted no better than the colour of the rods.' They went back from the island then with a great fear upon them.

THE WEIGHTY CALVES On the third day after that they took notice of another island, large and wide, and a herd in it of beautiful pigs, and they killed a young pig of them. But it was too weighty for them to lift it, so they all came around it and washed it and brought it into their boat. Then they saw a great mountain on the island, and Diuran the half-poet and German had a mind to go and to view the island from it. And when they came to the mountain, they found before them a broad river that was not deep; and German dipped the handle of his spear in the river and it was spent on the moment, as if fire had burned it, and so they went no farther. They saw them on the other side of the river great hornless oxen lying down and a very big man sitting with them; and German struck his spearshaft against his shield to frighten the cattle. 'Why

VOYAGE OF MAELDUNE

would you frighten these foolish calves?' said the big herdsman. 'Where are the dams of these calves?' said German. 'They are on the other side of the mountain beyond' said he. The two of them went back then to their comrades, and told them that news, and they said they would not go into the island, and they all went away.

THE MILL After that they found another island, and a great big ugly mill in it, and a miller, rough and ugly and withered, and they asked him what mill was this. 'It is the mill of the Inver of Trecenand' said he 'and everything that is begrudged is ground in it; and the half of the corn of this country is ground in this mill' he said. With that they saw heavy loads past all counting, and men and horses under them, coming to the mill and going from it again; and all that was brought from it was carried away westward. And when they heard and saw those things they blessed themselves with the sign of Christ's Cross and went again into their currach.

THE ISLAND OF KEENING When they went now from the island of the mill, they found a very large island and a great host of people in it. Black they were, both in their bodies and their clothing, and they had bands

BOOK FOUR: THE

around their heads, and they crying and ever-crying. And a lot fell by misfortune on one of the two fosterbrothers of Maeldune to land on the island. And no sooner did he reach to the people that were crying than he was as if one of them, and he began crying and lamenting the same as themselves. Then two of his comrades were sent to bring him out of that, and they could not make him out from the rest, and they bowed themselves down and cried along with them. Then Maeldune said 'Let four of you go with your weapons and bring back our men by force; and do not look at the ground or in the air, and put your cloaks over your nostrils and over your mouths, and do not breathe the air of the place, and do not take your eyes off your own men.' So the four went the way he told them and they brought back with them the other two. And when they were asked what had they seen in that country they would say 'We do not know that; but what we saw others doing, we did the same.' And they made haste to go away from that island.

THE FOUR-FENCED ISLAND   They came after that to another high island, having four fences in it that divided it into four parts. It is of gold the first fence was,

VOYAGE OF MAELDUNE

and another was of silver, and the third was brazen and the fourth of crystal. Kings there were in the one division, and queens in another; fighting men in another and young girls in the last. And one of the young girls went to meet them and brought them to land and gave them food that had the likeness of cheese, and whatever taste was pleasing to anyone, he would find that taste upon it. And she gave them drink from a little vessel, so that they slept in drunkenness for three days and three nights, and all that time the young girl was attending to them. And when they awoke on the third day they were in their boat at sea, and the island and the girl nowhere to be seen. And so they went on rowing.

THE WOMAN WITH THE PAIL Then they came to another little island, having a dun in it with a door of brass, and bolts of brass on the door. And there was a bridge of crystal to the door, and when they used to go upon that bridge they would fall down backwards. Then they saw a woman coming out from the dun, and a pail in her hand, and she lifted a slab of glass out from the bottom of the bridge, and she filled the pail from the well that was under the bridge, and went back again into the dun. 'It is a house-

BOOK FOUR: THE

keeper coming for Maeldune' said German. 'Maeldune indeed!' said she and she shut the door after her. They began then striking the fastenings and the net of brass that was before them, and the sound of them made sweet quieting music that put them into their sleep until the morning of the morrow. When they awoke they saw the same woman coming out of the dun, and her pail in her hand, and she filled it under the same slab. 'I tell you it is a housekeeper for Maeldune' said German. 'It is much I think of Maeldune!' said she, shutting the door of the liss after her. And when they struck at the door, the same music put them lying in their sleep till the morrow. They were that way through the length of three days and three nights; and on the fourth day the woman came to them, and it is beautiful she was coming. A white cloak she had on her, and a band of gold about her hair that was golden; two sandals of silver on her white-purple feet; a brooch of silver with bosses of gold in her cloak, a fine silk shirt next her white skin. 'My welcome to you Maeldune' said she, and she gave every man of them all his own name. 'It is long we have had knowledge and understanding of your coming here' she said. Then she brought

VOYAGE OF MAELDUNE

them with her into a great house that stood near the sea, and they drew up their currach on the strand. And they saw before them in the house a bed for Maeldune alone, and a bed for every three of his people. And she brought them in a basket food that was like curds, and she gave a share to every three, and whatever taste they wished to find on it they would find it; and as to Maeldune she served him by himself. And she filled her pail under the same slab and gave them out drink, the full of it for every three. And then she knew they had had their fill and she stopped from giving it out to them. 'A fitting wife for Maeldune this woman would be' said every one of his people. She went away from them then, and her vessel and her pail with her; and Maeldune's people said to him 'Will we ask her would she maybe be your wife?' 'What harm would it do you' said he 'to speak to her?' So when she came on the morrow they said to her 'Will you give your friendship to Maeldune and be his wife? And why would you not stop here to-night?' they said. But she said she did not know and had never known what marriage was; and she went from them to her own house.
On the morrow at the same time she came

BOOK FOUR: THE

to them; and when they had drunk and were satisfied they said the same words to her. 'To-morrow' she said 'you will get an answer to that.' She went to her own house then, and they went asleep on their beds. And when they awoke they were in their currach on a rock, and they did not see the island or the woman or the place where they had been.

THE SOUND LIKE PSALMS And as they went on they heard in the north-east a great shout and what was like the singing of psalms. And that night and the next day until nones, they were rowing till they could know what was that shout or that singing. Then they saw an island having high mountains full of birds, black and brown and speckled, calling and crying out very loud.

THE SOD FROM IRELAND They went on a little from that island, and they found another island of no great size, and a great many trees in it, and on them many birds. And in the island they saw a man and he clothed with his own hair, and they asked who was he and what was his race. 'It is of the men of Ireland I am' he said 'and I went on my pilgrimage in a little currach, and my currach split under me when I was gone a little way from land; and I went

VOYAGE OF MAELDUNE

back again to the land' he said 'and I put under my feet a sod of my own country, and on it I went out to sea. And the Lord settled down that sod for me in this place' he said 'and it is he adds a foot to its breadth every year from that time to this, and a tree every year to grow from it. And the birds you see in the trees' he said 'are the souls of my children and my kindred, women and men, that are there waiting for the day of judgment. Half a cake, and a bit of a fish, and a drink from the well, God has given me; and that comes to me every day' he said 'through the service of angels. And besides that' he said, 'at the hour of nones another half a cake and a bit of a fish come to every man and to every woman over there, and a drink out of the well that is enough for everyone.' And when their three nights of feasting were at an end they bade that man farewell, and he said to them 'You will all reach to your own country' he said 'but one man only.'

THE WELL OF NOURISHMENT The third day after that they found another island, and a golden wall around it, and the middle of it as white as feathers; and a man in it, and it is what he was clothed in, the hair of his own body. They asked him then what

BOOK FOUR: THE

nourishment he used. 'I will tell you the truth' he said 'there is a well in this island, and on a Friday and on a Wednesday whey or water is given out from it, and on Sunday and on the feasts of martyrs it is good milk is given out. But on the feasts of the apostles and of Mary and John Baptist, and on the high times of the year, it is beer and wine that it gives out.' At nones then there came to every man of them a cake and a bit of a fish, and they drank their fill of what came to them out of the well. And it cast them into a sleep of sleeping from that time until the morrow. And at the end of three nights the clerk bade them to go on. So they went on their way and bade him farewell.

THE SMITHS AT THE FORGE And when they had been a long time on the waves they saw an island a long way off, and as they came near it they heard the noise of smiths striking iron on the anvil with hammers, like the striking of three or four it was. And when they came near they heard one man say to another 'Are they near us?' 'They are near us' said the other. 'Who do you say are coming?' said another man. 'Little lads they seem to be in a little trough beyond' said he. When Maeldune heard what the smiths were saying

VOYAGE OF MAELDUNE

'Let us go back' he said; 'and let us not turn the boat but let her stern be foremost, the way they will not know us to be making away from them.' They rowed away then, and the stern of the boat foremost. And the same man said to the other in the forge 'Are they near the harbour now?' 'They are not stirring' said the man that was looking out. 'They do not come here and they do not go there' he said. It was not long after that he asked again 'What are they doing now?' 'It is what I think' said the man that was looking out 'that they are making away, for they are farther from the port now than they were a while ago.' Then the smith came out from the forge and a great lump of red-hot iron in the tongs in his hand, and he threw it after the boat into the sea, and the whole of the sea boiled up; but the iron did not reach to the currach, for they made away with their whole strength quickly and with no delay into the great ocean.

THE VERY CLEAR SEA   They went on after that till they came to a sea that was like glass, and so clear it was that the gravel and the sand of the sea could be seen through it, and they saw no beasts or no monsters at all among the rocks, but only the clean gravel and the grey sand. And through a great part

BOOK FOUR: THE

of the day they were going over that sea, and it is very grand it was and beautiful.

THE SEA LIKE A MIST   Then they put out into another sea that was like a cloud, and it seemed to them that it could not support themselves or the currach. And after that they saw below them walled duns and a beautiful country. And they saw a great terrible beast there, and he in a tree; and a herd of cattle round about the tree, and a man beside it, having shield and spear and sword; and when he saw the great beast that was in the tree he made away on the moment. And the beast stretched out its neck and stooped his head to the back of the ox that was biggest of the herd, and dragged it into the tree and had it eaten in the winking of an eye. On that the flocks and the herdsman made away; and when Maeldune and his people saw it there was greater dread again on them, for they thought they would never cross that sea without slipping down through it, and it as thin as a mist. But they got away over it after great danger.

THE PELTING WITH NUTS   After that they found another island, and the sea rose up around it making great cliffs of water on every side. And when the people of that

VOYAGE OF MAELDUNE

country saw them, they began screaming at them and saying 'It is they themselves! It is they themselves!' till they were out of breath, Then Maeldune and his men saw a great many people and great herds of cattle and of horses and a great many flocks of sheep. Then a woman began pelting them from below with great nuts that stopped floating on the waves about them, and they gathered up a good share of those nuts to bring away with them. And then they went back from the island, and with that the screams came to an end. 'Where are they now?' they heard a man saying that was coming towards them at the time of the screams. 'They are gone away' said another of them. 'They are not' said another. It is likely now the people of that island had a prophecy there would some person come that would destroy their country and drive them away out of it.

THE SALMON STREAM   They went on then to another island where a strange thing was showed to them, a great stream that rose up out of the strand, and that went like a bow of heaven over the whole of the island, and came down into the strand on the other side. And they were going under the stream without getting any wet, and they

BOOK FOUR: THE

were piercing the stream above, and very large salmon were falling from the stream above on to the ground of the island. And the whole of the island was full of the smell of the salmon, for there was no one could come to an end of taking them because of their number. And from the evening of Sunday until the full light of the Monday that stream did not move, but stopped in its silence where it was in the sea. Then they brought together the biggest of the salmon into one place, and they filled their currach with them and went away over the ocean.

THE SILVER-MESHED NET They went on then till they found a great silver pillar; four sides it had and the width of each of the sides was two strokes of an oar; and there was not one sod of earth about it, but only the endless ocean; and they could not see what way it was below, and they could not see what way the top of it was because of its height. There was a silver net from the top of it that spread out a long way on every side, and the currach went under sail through a mesh of that net. Then Diuran gave a blow of his spear at the mesh. 'Do not destroy the net' said Maeldune 'for we are looking at the work of great men.' 'It is

VOYAGE OF MAELDUNE

for the praise of God's name I am doing it' said Diuran 'the way my story will be the better believed; and it is to the altar of Ardmacha I will give this mesh of the net if I get back to Ireland.' Two ounces and a half now was the weight of it when it was measured after in Ardmacha. They heard then a voice from the top of the pillar very loud and clear, but they did not know in what strange language it was speaking or what word it said.

THE DOOR UNDER LOCKS They saw then another island having one foot supporting it. And they rowed around looking for a way to come into it and finding none; but they saw down at the bottom of the foot a closed door under locks, and they understood it was by that way the island was entered. And they saw a plough on the height of the island, but they spoke with no one and no one spoke with them and they went on their way.

THE BALL OF THREAD They came after that to an island having a great plain in it, without any heath but smooth and grassy. And they saw a great dun near the sea, high and strong, and a large house, roofed and having good beds in it, and seventeen

BOOK FOUR: THE

girls were in it making ready a bath. They landed then on that island and sat down on a hill before the gate of the dun, and it is what Maeldune said: 'We may be sure it is for us that bath is being made ready.' At the hour of nones they saw a woman on a horse of victory coming to the dun. A well ornamented cloth she had under her, and a blue embroidered hood on her head; a fringed crimson cloak, gloves worked with gold on her hands and beautiful sandals on her feet. As she got down one of the young girls took her horse, and she went in then to the dun and into the bath. And it was not long until a girl of the girls came to them. 'Your coming is welcome' she said 'and come now into the dun, it is the queen is asking you.' So they went into the dun and they all washed in the bath; and after that the queen was sitting on one side of the house and her seventeen girls around her; and Maeldune was sitting on the other side, near the queen, and his seventeen men around him. Then a dish of good food was brought to Maeldune, and a vessel of glass that was full of good drink, and a dish and a vessel for every three of his people. And they all stopped there that night in the seven-

VOYAGE OF MAELDUNE

teen covered rooms of the house and Maeldune slept with the queen. And when they rose up in the morning the queen said 'Let you stop here' she said 'and age will not fall on you beyond the age you are found in at this time; and you will have lasting life for ever' she said 'and what you got last night you will get for ever without any labour; and give up this wandering from island to island of the sea' she said. 'Tell us' said Maeldune 'what way are you here?' 'It is not hard to say that' she said. 'There was a good man in this place, the king of the island; and I bore him seventeen daughters, and I was their mother. And then he died and left no man to inherit after him, and I myself took the kingship of the island. And every day' she said 'I go into the great plain there beyond to give out judgments and to settle the disputes of the people.' 'Why would you go from us to-day?' said Maeldune. 'Unless I go' she said 'what happened us last night will not happen us again. And you may stop in your house' she said, 'and there is no need for you to work, and I will go judge the people on behalf of you.' They stopped in that island through the three months of the winter, and they seemed to them to be three years.

BOOK FOUR: THE

'It is long we are here' said a man of Maeldune's people to him then. 'And why do we not go back to our own country?' he said. 'What you are saying is not right' said Maeldune 'for we will not find in our own country any better thing than what we are getting here.' His people began to murmur greatly against him then, and it is what they said: 'It is great love he has for his wife. And let him stop with her if he has a mind' they said 'and we will go to our own country.' 'I will not stop here after you' said Maeldune. One day now the queen went to the judging where she went every day, and no sooner was she gone than they went into their currach. But she came on her horse and she threw a ball of thread after them, and Maeldune caught it, and it held to his hand, and a thread of the ball was in her own hand, and she drew back the boat to the harbour and to herself with that thread. They stopped with her then for another three months, and then they made away and she brought them back with a thread the same as she did before, and three times that happened to them. And they consulted among themselves then and it is what they said: 'It is certain' they said 'it is great love Maeldune has for this woman; and

VOYAGE OF MAELDUNE

it is by reason of that he catches the ball of thread the way it will hold to his hand, and the way we will be brought back to the dun.' 'Let some other one take the thread next time' said Maeldune; 'and if it holds in his hand let the hand be cut off him' he said. So they went on then to their boat, and the queen came and she threw the ball after them, and some man in the currach caught it, and it held to his hand. Then Diuran struck his hand off, and it fell and the thread with it into the sea. And when the queen saw that she began to cry and to call out till the whole island was one loud cry and one lament. And in that way they made their escape from her out of the island.

THE SALLEY TREES   For a long while after that they were driven about on the waves, till they found an island having trees on it like salley trees or hazel, and large wonderful berries on the trees. So they stripped a little tree and they cast lots who should try the berries, and the lot fell upon Maeldune. He squeezed some of the berries then into the vessel and drank, and it put him into a deep sleep from that hour to the same hour on the morrow; and they did not know was he alive or dead, and the red foam around his lips, till

BOOK FOUR: THE

he awoke on the morrow. He said to them then 'Let you gather' he said 'this fruit, for it is great the good there is in it.' So they gathered all there was of it, and they were squeezing it and filling all the vessels they had with them, and they mixed water with the juice to lessen the sleep of its drunkenness. And after that was done they rowed away from that island.

THE BIRD THAT GOT BACK ITS YOUTH   After that they stopped at another large island, the one side of it a wood having yews and great oaks in it, and the other side a plain having a little lake; and they saw great flocks of sheep on the plain. And they saw a little church and a dun and they went to the church, and there was an old grey priest in it, and he clothed entirely in his own hair. 'Eat now your fill of the sheep' he said 'and do not use more than is enough.' So they stopped there for a while, and fed upon the flesh of the sheep. One day now as they were looking out from the island, they saw a cloud coming towards them from the south-west. And after a while as they were looking they knew it to be a bird, for they could see its wings moving. Then it came into the island and lit upon a hill near the lake, and it is what they thought,

VOYAGE OF MAELDUNE

it would carry them in its claws out to sea. And it had with it a branch of a great tree, and the branch was bigger than one of the great oaks, and it had twigs on it, and a plenty of heavy fruit, and the top of it full of fresh leaves. And Maeldune and his men were in hiding watching what would the bird do. And by reason that it was tired it stopped quiet for a while, and then it began to eat the fruit of the tree. So Maeldune went on till he was at the edge of the hill where the bird was, to see would it do him any harm, and it did not meddle with him, and then all his people followed him to that place. 'Let one of us go' said Maeldune 'and gather some of the fruit that is before the bird.' So a man of them went then and he gathered a share of the berries, and the bird made no complaint and did not look at him or make any stir at all. And then all of them went behind it, and their shields with them, and it did them no harm. And towards the hour of nones they saw two eagles in the south-west, in the same quarter the great bird had come from, and they pitched in front of the great bird. And when they had stopped quiet for a good while they began to take off the lice that were about the great bird's jaws and its eyes and its ears.

BOOK FOUR: THE

They went on doing that till vespers, and the three of them began to eat the berries of the branch. And from the morning of the morrow till the middle of the day they were picking at the great bird in the same way, and stripping the old feathers from it and the scabs. But when midday came they began to strip the berries from the branch, and they were crushing them against the stones with their beaks and throwing them into the lake till the foam of it turned to be red. After that the great bird went into the lake and he was washing himself there till towards the end of the day. After that he went out of the lake and pitched in another place on the same hill, the way the lice that were picked out of him would not settle on him again. And on the morning of the morrow the same two eagles dressed and smoothed the feathers of the great bird as if it was done with a comb, and they kept at that until midday, and then they went away the same way as they had come. But the great bird stopped after them shaking out his wings and his feathers till the end of the third day. And at the hour of tierce on the third day he rose up and flew three times round the island, and then he pitched for a little rest on the same hill, and after that he

VOYAGE OF MAELDUNE

rose and went away far off towards the southwest where he came from, and it is swifter and stronger his flight was that time than when he came. They all knew then that had been his renewing from old age to youth, after the word of the prophet that said 'Thy youth shall be renewed like the eagle's.' It is then Diuran said, seeing that great wonder, 'Let us go' he said 'into the lake to renew ourselves the same as the bird.' 'Do not' said another 'for the bird has left his poison in it.' 'It is not right what you are saying' said Diuran 'and I will go into it first myself' he said. He went in then and bathed himself there and put his lips into the water and he drank sups of it. It is young and strong his eyes were after that so long as he was living, and he never lost a tooth or a hair from his head, and he was never sick or sorry from that out. They bade farewell then to their old man and they took a share of the sheep with them for provision, and then they put out their boat and they went on over the ocean.

THE LAUGH- Then they found another
ING PEOPLE island, and a wide level plain in it, and a great crowd of people on that plain, and they playing and laughing without end. They cast lots then who would

go and search out the island, and the lot fell on the head of the third of Maeldune's foster-brothers. And no sooner did he land on the island than he began to play and to laugh along with the people that were on it, as if he had been one of them from the beginning. And his comrades stopped for a long time waiting for him and he never came back to them; so they left him there.

THE FIRE-WALLED ISLAND   After that they saw another island that was no great size, and a fiery wall round about it, and that wall used to move round and round the island. There was an open door, now, in the side of the wall, and whenever the door would come opposite them, they used to see the whole island and all that was in it, and all the people of it, that were beautiful and wearing embroidered clothes, and golden vessels in their hands, and they feasting. And they could hear the ale-music those people were making. And they were for a long time looking at that wonder, and it is delightful they thought it.

THE COVETOUS COOK   They were not long gone from that island when they saw far off among the waves a shape like a white bird, and they turned the prow of

VOYAGE OF MAELDUNE

the boat southward, till they would see what was it. And when they were come near they saw it was a man, and he clothed only with the white hair of his body, and he was throwing himself and stretching himself upon a wide rock. When they were come to him they asked a blessing of him, and they asked where he had come from to that rock. 'It is from Toraig I am come surely' he said 'and it is in Toraig I was reared. And it is what happened, I was a cook in it, and it is a bad cook I was, for I used to be selling for means and for treasures for myself the food of the church where I was, so that my house grew to be full of quilts and of pillows and of clothes, both linen and woollen, of every colour, and of pails of brass and of silver, and brooches of silver having pins of gold, the way there was nothing wanting in my house of all that is thought much of by men, both of golden books and of bags for books, that were ornamented with silver and gold. And I used to be digging under the houses of the church, and I brought many treasures out of them; and it is great was my pride and my boasting. One day, now, I was bade to dig a grave for the body of a countryman that had been brought into the island, and as I was at the grave I heard

BOOK FOUR: THE

a voice that was coming up under my feet. "Do not dig in that place" it said; "Do not put the body of a sinner upon me, a holy, religious person." "I will put it between myself and God" said I in the greatness of my pride. "If that is so" said the voice "your mouth shall perish on the third day from this, and it is in hell you will be, and the body will not stop here." "What good will you give me if I do not lay the body upon you?" said I. "To have lasting life with God" said he. "How can I know that?" said I. "That is not hard for you" said he. "The grave you are digging now will be full of sand, and it will be showed to you by that you cannot lay the body upon me however much you may try;" and those words were hardly said when the grave was full of sand. So after that I buried the body in another place. One time, now, I put out a new currach, having red hide over it, on the sea. And I went into the currach and I was well pleased to be looking about me. And I left nothing in my house, small or great, without bringing it with me, of vats and of drinking vessels and of horns. And while I was looking at the sea, and it calm for me, great winds came upon me and brought me away in to the sea till I did not see land nor ground. And then

VOYAGE OF MAELDUNE

my currach stayed still, and from that out it did not stir from the place where it was. And as I was looking about me on every side I saw to my right hand the man that had spoken from the grave, and he sitting on the waves, and it is what he said to me "Where are you going?" he said. "I like well" I said "the view I have over the sea." "You would not like it well" he said "if you could see the troop that is about you." "What troop is that?" said I. "There is nothing so far as your sight reaches over the sea and up to the clouds," he said, "but one troop of demons all around you, by reason of your covetousness and your vanity and your pride and your theft and your other bad deeds. And do you know why it is your boat is stopping where it is?" "I do not know that indeed" said I. "The currach will not go out of the place where it is," he said, "until such time as you will do my bidding." "Maybe I will not put up with it" said I. "You will give in to the pains of hell unless you give in to my will" said he. He came towards me then, and laid his hand upon me and I said I would do his bidding. "Put out" he said "into the sea all the riches you have stored in the boat." "It would be a pity" said I "that all should go to loss." "It will not go to loss"

BOOK FOUR: THE

said he, "there is one will get profit by it." I threw out then into the sea all that was in the boat but one small wooden cup. "Go on now out of this" he said "and whatever place your currach stops let you stay in that place." And he gave me provision then, the full of the cup of whey water, and seven cakes. So I went on then' said the old man 'where my currach and the wind brought me for I had let my oars and the rudder go from me. And as I was moving about upon the waves I was cast upon this rock, and I was in doubt if the boat had stopped for I saw neither land nor ground. And I brought to mind then what had been said to me, to stop in the place where my boat would stop. So I raised myself up and I saw a little rock and the waves laughing about it. Then I set my foot on the little rock, and the rock lifted me up and the waves went from it. Seven years I was here' he said 'having but the seven cakes, and at the end of that time the cakes failed me and I had but the cup of whey water. And after I had fasted three days, at the hour of nones an otter brought a salmon to me out of the sea. And I said to myself in my mind I would never be satisfied to eat the salmon raw, and I put it out again into the sea; and I was fasting

VOYAGE OF MAELDUNE

through the length of another three days. And at the third none I saw the otter bringing the salmon to me again out of the sea; and another otter brought kindled wood and put it down and blew it with his breath that the fire blazed up. So I roasted the salmon, and for another seven years I lived that way. And a salmon would come to me every day' he said 'and with it firing, and the rock was increasing until now it is large. And at the end of the seven years' he said 'my salmon was not given to me, and I was fasting through another three days. And at the third none there were put up to me the half a wheaten cake and a bit of a fish. Then my cup of whey water went from me, and there came to me a cup of the same size that was full of good drink, and it is here on the rock and it full every day. And neither wind nor wet nor heat nor cold vexes me in this place. And that is my story for you' said the old man. And when the hour of none was come the half of a cake and a bit of a fish came for every man of them, and in the cup that was on the rock with the old man there was their full of good drink. The old man said to them then 'You will all reach to your country, and the man that killed your father, Maeldune,

BOOK FOUR: THE

you will find him before you in a dun; and do not kill him, but give him forgiveness since God has saved you from many great dangers, and you yourselves are deserving of death the same as himself.' They bade farewell then to the old man, and they went on as they were used to do; And as to the commandment he had given, it is well Maeldune kept it in mind and obeyed it afterwards.

THE BIRD FROM IRELAND

After they were gone from that now, they came to an island having in it a great many cattle, oxen and cows and sheep, but there were no houses in it or duns. They ate the flesh of the sheep, and one of them said then, and he looking at a large bird, 'That bird is like the birds of Ireland.' 'That is true indeed' said some of the rest. 'Keep a watch on it' said Maeldune 'and see what way will it go from us.' They saw then the bird flying from them to the south-east, and they rowed after it in that direction and they went on rowing until vespers, and at the fall of night they came in sight of land that was like the land of Ireland. And they rowed towards it, and they found a small island and it was from that island the wind had brought them into the ocean the time they first put out to sea. They

VOYAGE OF MAELDUNE

drew their boat on shore then and they went to the dun that was in the island, and they were listening to the people of the dun that were at their supper at that time. And it is what they heard some of them saying 'It will be well for us if we never see Maeldune again.' 'It is drowned Maeldune was' said another man of them. 'If he should come in now' said another 'what should we do?' 'It is not hard to say that' said the man of the house. 'There would be a great welcome before him if he should come, for it is a long time he has been under great hardship.' With that Maeldune struck the hand-wood against the door. 'Who is there?' said the doorkeeper. 'Maeldune is here.' 'Open the door then' said the man of the house 'for it is welcome your coming is.' They came into the house then, and there was a great welcome before them and new clothing was given to them. Then they bore witness to all the wonders God had showed to them, after the word of the holy hymn that said

Hæc olim meminisse juvabit.

And then Maeldune went to his own district, and Diuran the half-poet took the five half ounces of silver he had taken from the net

THE VOYAGE OF MAELDUNE

and laid them on the altar of Ardmacha in joy and in triumph at the miracles and great wonders God had done for them. And they told their journey from beginning to end, and all the troubles and dangers they had found by land and by sea.

Aedh Finn, now, chief story teller of Ireland put down this story the way it is here; for gladdening the mind he did it and for the people of Ireland after him.

BOOK FIVE:
GREAT WONDERS OF THE OLDEN TIME.

BLESSED CIARAN AND HIS SCHOLARS The first of the saints to be born in Ireland of the saints was Ciaran, that was of the blood of the nobles of Leinster. And the first of the wonders he did was in the island of Cleire, and he but a young child at the time. There came a hawk in the air over his head, and it stooped down before him and took up a little bird that was sitting on a nest. And pity for the little bird came on Ciaran and it was bad to him the way it was. And the hawk turned back and left the bird before him, and it half dead and trembling; and Ciaran bade it to rise up and it rose and went up safe and well to its nest, by the grace of God. It was Patrick bade Ciaran after that to go to the Well of Uaran, the mering where the north meets with the south in the middle part of Ireland. 'And bring my little bell with you' he said 'and it will be without speaking till you come to the Well.' So Ciaran did that and when he reached to the Well of Uaran, for God brought him there, the little bell spoke out on the moment in a bright clear voice. And Ciaran settled himself there, and he alone, and great woods all around the place; and he

BOOK FIVE: GREAT WONDERS

began to make a little cell for himself, that was weak enough. And one time as he was sitting under the shadow of a tree a wild boar rose up on the other side of it; but when it saw Ciaran it ran from him, and then it turned back again as a quiet servant to him, being made gentle by God. And that boar was the first scholar and the first monk Ciaran had; and it used to be going into the wood and to be plucking rods and thatch between its teeth as if to help towards the building. And there came wild creatures to Ciaran out of the places where they were, a fox and a badger and a wolf and a doe; and they were tame with him and humbled themselves to his teaching the same as brothers, and did all he bade them to do. But one day the fox, that was greedy and cunning and full of malice, met with Ciaran's brogues and he stole them and went away shunning the rest of the company to his own old den, for he had a mind to eat the brogues. But that was showed to Ciaran, and he sent another monk of the monks of his family, that was the badger, to bring back the fox to the place where they all were. So the badger went to the cave where the fox was and found him, and he after eating the thongs and the ears of the brogues And the badger would

OF THE OLDEN TIME

not let him off coming back with him to Ciaran, and they came to him in the evening bringing the brogues with them. And Ciaran said to the fox 'O brother' he said ' why did you do this robbery that was not right for a monk to do? And there was no need for you to do it' he said 'for we all have food and water in common, that there is no harm in. But if your nature told you it was better for you to use flesh, God would have made it for you from the bark of those trees that are about you.' Then the fox asked Ciaran to forgive him and to put a penance on him; and Ciaran did that, and the fox used no food till such time as he got leave from Ciaran; and from that out he was as honest as the rest.

HIS KINDNESS IS LIVING YET   It is not long since a poor woman of Aidne that used to be doing spinning for the neighbours, and that had a little son that was lame, brought him to a blessed well of Ciaran.   And when they looked in it they saw a little fish tossing and leaping and the water bubbling up, and a woman that was there said 'It is many years I am coming here, and I never saw that fish until now.' And from that time the lameness went from the little lad. And there was a poor

BOOK FIVE: GREAT WONDERS

woman in Iar Connacht was fretting greatly because she was told that her son that was in America had lost his leg through a train. And she thought maybe she did not hear all the truth, and that the neighbours might be hiding from her that he was dead. So she went to a well of blessed Ciaran and she kneeled down on the stones, and she prayed three times to God and to the saint to give her a sign. And at the third time a little fish rose up and went swimming and stirring itself at the top of the water as if to show itself, and she saw that a piece had been taken out of it and that it was lively all the same. And sure enough her son got well and is living in America yet. And many that have some belonging to them across the ocean will go and ask for a sign at that well, and it will be given to them the same as it was to her.

BLESSED CELL- The time Cellach, that
ACH'S LAMENT was a saint of Connacht and a son of the king, was taken by his enemies they put him in a hollow of an oak tree for the night. And he made this complaint, and he waiting for his death: 'My blessing to the morning that is as white as a flame; my blessing to Him that sends it, the brave new morning; my blessing to you white proud

OF THE OLDEN TIME

morning, sister to the bright sun; morning that lights up my little book for me.

'It is you are the guest in every house; it is you shine on every race and every family; white-necked morning, gold-clear, wonderful.

'Och, scallcrow, Och, scallcrow, grey-cloaked, sharpbeaked; it is well I know your desire; you are no friend to Cellach!

'Och, raven doing your croaking; if there is hunger on you do not leave this place till you get your fill of my flesh!

'The kite of the Yew Tree of Cluan Eo, it is he will be rough in the struggle; he will take the full of his grey claws; it is not in kindness he will part from me!

'Little wren of the scanty tail, it is a pity the song you gave; it is surely for betraying you are come and for the shortening of my life.

'The red fox will come hurrying when he hears the blows upon me; the wolf from the eastern side of the Ridge of the son of Dara.

'The great Son of Mary is saying over my head "You will have earth, you will have Heaven; there is a welcome before you Cellach!"'

THE WOLF'S PROPHECY It chanced one day not long after the coming of the Gall from England into Ireland, there was a priest

BOOK FIVE: GREAT WONDERS

making his way through a wood of Meath. And there came a man fornenst him and bade him for the love of God to come with him to confess his wife that was lying sick near that place. So the priest turned with him and it was not long before he heard groaning and complaining as would be heard from a woman, but when he came where she was lying it was a wolf he saw before him on the ground. The priest was afeared when he saw that and he turned away; but the man and the wolf spoke with him and bade him not to be afeared but to turn and to confess her. Then the priest took heart and blessed him and sat down beside her. And the wolf spoke to him and made her confession to the priest and he anointed her. And when they had that done, the priest began to think in himself that she that had that mislikeness upon her and had grace to speak, might likely have grace and the gift of knowledge in other things; and he asked her about the strangers that were come into Ireland, and what way it would be with them. And it is what the wolf said: 'It was through the sin of the people of this country Almighty God was displeased with them and sent that race to bring them into bondage, and so they must be until the

OF THE OLDEN TIME

Gall themselves will be encumbered with sin. And at that time the people of Ireland will have power to put on them the same wretchedness for their sins.'

LIBAN THE SEA WOMAN The time Angus Og sent away Eochaid and Ribh from the plain of Bregia that was his playing ground, he gave them the loan of a very big horse to carry all they had northward. And Eochaid went on with the horse till he came to the Grey Thornbush in Ulster; and a well broke out where he stopped, and he made his dwelling-house beside it, and he made a cover for the well and put a woman to mind it. But one time she did not shut down the cover, and the water rose up and covered the Grey Thornbush, and Eochaid was drowned with his children; and the water spread out into a great lake that has the name of Loch Neach to this day. But Liban that was one of Eochaid's daughters was not drowned, but she was in her sunny-house under the lake and her little dog with her for a full year, and God protected her from the waters. And one day she said 'O Lord, it would be well to be in the shape of a salmon, to be going through the sea the way they do.' Then the one half of her took the shape of a salmon and the other half

BOOK FIVE: GREAT WONDERS

kept the shape of a woman; and she went swimming the sea, and her little dog following her in the shape of an otter and never leaving her or parting from her at all. And one time Caoilte was out at a hunting near Beinn Boirche with the King of Ulster, and they came to the shore of the sea. And when they looked out over it they saw a young girl on the waves, and she swimming with the side-stroke and the foot-stroke. And when she came opposite them she sat up on a wave, as anyone would sit upon a stone or a hillock and she lifted her head and she said 'Is not that Caoilte Son of Ronan?' 'It is myself surely' said he. 'It is many a day' she said 'we saw you upon that rock, and the best man of Ireland or of Scotland with you, that was Finn son of Cumhal. 'Who are you so girl?' said Caoilte. 'I am Liban daughter of Eochaid, and I am in the water these hundred years, and I never showed my face to anyone since the going away of the King of the Fianna to this day. And it is what led me to lift my head to-day' she said 'was to see yourself Caoilte.' Just then the deer that were running before the hounds made for the sea and swam out into it. 'Your spear to me Caoilte!' said Liban. Then he put the spear into her hand and she

OF THE OLDEN TIME

killed the deer with it, and sent them back to him where he was with the King of Ulster; and then she threw him back the spear and with that she went away. And that is the way she was until the time Beoan son of Innle was sent by Comgall to Rome, to have talk with Gregory and to bring back rules and orders. And when he and his people were going over the sea they heard what was like the singing of angels under the currach. 'What is that song?' said Beoan. 'It is I myself am making it' said Liban. 'Who are you?' said Beoan. 'I am Liban daughter of Eochaid son of Mairid, and I am going through the sea these three hundred years.' Then she told him all her story, and how it was under the round hulls of ships she had her dwelling-place, and the waves were the roofing of her house, and the strands its walls. 'And it is what I am come for now' she said 'to tell you that I will come to meet you on this day twelve-month at Inver Ollorba; and do not fail to meet me there for the sake of all the saints of Dalaradia.' And at the year's end the nets were spread along the coast where she said she would come, and it was in the net of Fergus from Miluic she was taken. And the clerks gave her her choice either to be bap-

BOOK FIVE: GREAT WONDERS

tized and go then and there to heaven, or to stay living through another three hundred years and at the end of that time to go to heaven; and the choice she made was to die. Then Comgall baptized her and the name he gave her was Muirgheis, the Birth of the Sea. So she died, and the messengers that came and that carried her to her burying place, were horned deer that were sent by the angels of God.'

THE PRIEST AND THE BEES   There was a good honourable well-born priest, God's darling he was, a man holding to the yoke of Christ; and it happened he went one day to attend on a sick man. And as he was going a swarm of bees came towards him, and he having the Blessed Body of Christ with him there. And when he saw the swarm he laid the Blessed Body on the ground and gathered the swarm into his bosom, and went on in that way upon his journey, and forgot the Blessed Body where he had laid it. And after a while the bees went back from him again, and they found the Blessed Body and carried it away between them to their own dwelling place, and they gave honour to it kindly and made a good chapel of wax for it, and an altar and a chalice and a pair of priests,

OF THE OLDEN TIME

shaping them well out of wax to stand before Christ's Body. But as for the priest, when he remembered it he went looking for it carefully, penitently, and could not find it in any place. And it went badly with him and he went to confession, and with the weight of the trouble that took hold of him he was fretting through the length of a year. And there came an angel to him at the end of the year and told him the way the Body of Christ was sheltered and honoured. And the angel bade him to bring all the people to see that wonder; and they went there and when they saw it a great many of them believed.

THE HYMN OF MOLLING'S GUEST As Molling, saint of the Gael, was praying in his church one time, he saw a young man coming to him into the house. A comely shape he had and purple clothing about him. 'Good be with you, Clerk' he said. 'Amen' said Molling. 'Why do you give me no blessing?' said the young man. 'Who are you?' said Molling. 'I am Jesus Christ the Son of God.' 'That is not so' said Molling. 'In the time Christ used to come and to be talking with the servants of God, it is not in purple or like a king he was, but it is in the shape of the miserable the poor and the lepers he

BOOK FIVE: GREAT WONDERS

used to come.' 'If it is not believing me you are' said the young man 'who is it you think I am?' 'In my opinion' said Molling 'it is the devil you are, coming for my hurt.' 'It is harmful to you your unbelief is' said the young man. 'Well' said Molling 'here is your successor, the Gospel of Christ' and with that he raised up the book. 'Do not raise it up Clerk' said the young man then; 'for it is likely I am what you say, the man full of trouble.' 'For what cause are you come?' said Molling. 'To ask a blessing of you' said he. 'I will not give it' said Molling; 'for it is not a blessing you would be the better of. And what good would it be to you?' he said. 'O Clerk' said the young man 'it would be like as if you would go into a vat of honey and your clothing on you, and bathe yourself in it, the smell of it would be about you unless you would wash your clothing.' 'I will not give it to you' said Molling 'for it is not your true desire.' 'Well' he said 'give me the full of a curse.' 'What good will that do you?' said Molling. 'Not hard to say that, Clerk; if your mouth should give out the curse on me, its hurt & its poison would be on your lips.' 'Go' said Molling 'you are worthy of no blessing.' 'It would be best for me to earn it'

OF THE OLDEN TIME

said he; 'and what way can I do that?' 'By serving God' said Molling. 'My grief' he said 'I cannot do that.' 'By fasting then.' 'I am fasting since the beginning of the world' he said 'and I am none the better for it.' 'Bow your knees' said Molling. 'I cannot do that for it is turned backwards my knees are.' 'Go out from this' said Molling 'for I cannot save you.' And it is what the stranger said then:

'He is clean gold, he is Heaven about the sun, he is a silver vessel having wine in it; he is an angel, he is the wisdom of saints; everyone that is doing the will of the King.

'He is a bird with a trap closing about him; he is a broken ship in great danger; he is an empty vessel, he is a withered tree; he that is not doing the will of the King.

'He is a sweet-smelling branch with its blossoms; he is a vessel that is full of honey; he is a shining stone of good luck; he who does the will of the Son of God of heaven.

'He is a blind nut without profit; he is ill-smelling rottenness, he is a withered tree; he is a wild apple branch without blossom; he that is not doing the will of the King.

'If he does the will of the Son of God of Heaven, he is a bright sun with summer

BOOK FIVE: GREAT WONDERS

about it; he is the image of the God of Heaven; he is a vessel of clear glass.

'He is a racehorse over a smooth plain, the man that is striving for the kingdom of the great God; he is a chariot that is seen under a king, that wins the victory with golden bridles.

'He is a sun that warms high heaven; the king to whom the great King is thankful; he is a church, joyful, noble; he is a shrine having gold about it.

'He is an altar having wine poured upon it; having many quires singing around; he is a clean chalice with ale in it; he is bronze, white, shining; he is gold.'

TUAN, SON OF CAIRELL   Finnen of Magh Bile, saint of the Gael, went one time into Ulster to a rich fighting-man that had no good belief and that would not let him or his people into his house, but left them fasting through the Sunday. Then there came to them a very old clerk and bade them to come with him. 'Come to my dwelling-place' he said 'for it will be more fitting for you.' They went with him then, and they went through the duties of the Lord's day with psalms and with preachings and with offerings. Then Finnen asked him his name. 'I am one of the

OF THE OLDEN TIME

men of Ulster' he said 'and I am now Tuan son of Cairell; but Tuan grandson of Sera, son of Partholon's brother, that was my name at the first.' Then Finnen bade him to tell all that had happened in Ireland from the time of Partholon, and they said they would not eat with him until he had told them the stories of Ireland. 'It is hard not to be thinking of the word of God you have been giving out to us' said Tuan. But Finnen said 'You have leave to tell us now your own story, and the story of Ireland. 'Five times' he said then 'Ireland was taken after the flood; and then Partholon and his people took it, and between two Sundays a sickness came upon them, that they all died but one man only. But it is not the custom for destruction to come without one coming out of it to tell the story, and I myself am that one' he said. 'After that I was going from hill to hill and from cliff to cliff, keeping myself from wolves through two and twenty years, and all Ireland empty. Then the withering of age came upon me, and I was in waste places and my walk failed me, and I took caves for myself. Then Nemed my father's brother came into Ireland with his people, and I saw them from the cliffs, and I was avoiding them, and I hairy,

BOOK FIVE: GREAT WONDERS

clawed, withered, grey, naked, sorrowful, miserable. Then one night in my sleep I saw myself going into the shape of a stag, and I was in that shape, and young and glad in my mind. And there grew upon my head two antlers having three score points, and I was the leader of the herds of Ireland, and there was a great herd of stags about me whatever way I went. That is the way I spent my life through the time of Nemed and his race, but they all died in the end. Then the withering of age came upon me again, and I was going away from men and from wolves. One time I was at the door of my cave, I remember it yet, I knew I was going from one shape into another. It was into the shape of a wild boar I went and it is what I said:

'I am a boar to-day among many; I am a king looking for victories; the King of all has put me in hard trouble under many shapes. When I was at Dun Bre in the mornings fighting against old fighting men, it is comely my troop was beyond the pool; a beautiful host was following me.

'It is swift my troop was, going in revenge among armies; throwing my spears on every side against the hosts of Inisfail.

'When we were in the gathering giving out

OF THE OLDEN TIME

the judgments of Partholon it was sweet to everyone what I said; those were the words that went very close.

'It is sweet was my pleasant judgment among the beautiful women; stately my comely chariot; sweet my singing across a dark plain.

'It is swift was my step without straying in the first rush of the battles; it is comely my face was that day; to-day it is the dark face of a boar.

'For it was in that shape I was truly' he said 'and I was young and glad in my mind, and I was the king of the boar-herds of Ireland, and I went the round of my dwelling when I came into the district of Ulster; for it was in that place I changed into all those shapes, and it is to that place I came for renewing in the time of my withering and my misery. Then Semion son of Stariath and his people took this island. From them are the Fir Domnann and the Firbolg and the Galliana, and all these lived their time in Ireland. And age came upon me, and my mind was troubled, and I could not do the things I was used to. And I went back to my own place, and I remembered every shape I was in before, and I fasted my three days as I had always done,

BOOK FIVE: GREAT WONDERS

and I had no strength left. And after that I went into the shape of a great hawk and my mind was glad again, I was able to do everything; and I said to myself that dearer to me every day was God, the Friend who had shaped me. Then Beothach son of Iarbonel the prophet took this island from the races that were in it. From them are the Tuatha De Danaan and the An-De; and where they came from the learned do not know, but it seems to them likely they came from heaven, because of their skill and the excellence of their knowledge. I was a long time in the shape of that hawk till I outlived all the races that had taken the land of Ireland. Then the sons of Miled took the island by force from the Tuatha De Danaan, and I was in the shape of that hawk yet, and I was in the hollow of a tree on a river. It is sorrowful my mind was; all the birds came to me quietly. There I fasted three days and three nights and sleep fell upon me, and I went there and then into the shape of a salmon, and God put me into the river and I was in it. It is well content I was then and strong and well nourished, and it is good my swimming was, and I used to escape from every net and every danger, from the claws of hawks and from the hands

OF THE OLDEN TIME

fishermen and their spears; and the marks of everyone of them are on me yet. And when God, my help, thought it time, and when the beasts were following me and I was known to every fisherman in every pool, the fisherman of Cairell, king of that country, took me and brought me to the queen, I remember it well; the man put me on a spit and roasted me, and the queen, that had a desire for fish, eat me so that I was in her womb. I remember well the time I was in her womb and what each one said to her in the house, and all that was done in Ireland through that time. I remember after my birth when speech came to me as it comes to every person, and I knew all that was going on in Ireland, and I was a seer and they gave me the name of Tuan son of Cairell. After that, Patrick came with the faith to Ireland and I was baptized and believed in the only King of all things and of the Elements.' And after Tuan had told that, Finnen and his people stopped there through a week talking with him. And every history and every genealogy that is in Ireland, it is from him it comes; or if not from him, then from Fintain, that Tuan said was older again than himself, as he was; being son of Bochra, son of Bith, son of Noah.

BOOK FIVE: GREAT WONDERS

FINTAIN'S YEW TREE And when Fintain came to Ireland is not known; but anyway it was for him and for Tuan that Diarmuid King of Teamhuir sent one time when there was a dispute about land and about the old custom. And when Fintain came he had eighteen troops with him, nine before him and nine after him, that were all of them his children's children. And when the king's people asked how far did his memory go back 'I will tell you that' he said. 'I passed one day through the west of Munster, and I brought home with me a red berry of a yew tree and I planted it in my garden and it grew there till it was the height of a man. I took it out of the garden then and I planted it in the green lawn before my house, and it grew in that lawn till a hundred fighting men could come together under its branches, and find shelter there from wind and rain and cold and heat. And I myself and my yew tree were wearing out our time together, till at last all the leaves withered and fell from it. And then to get some profit from it I cut it down and I made from it seven vats, seven kieves, seven barrels, seven churns, seven pitchers, seven measures, seven methers, with hoops for all. I went on then with my yew vessels till the hoops fell

OF THE OLDEN TIME

from them with age and rottenness. After that I made them over again, but all I could get was a kieve out of the vat, a barrel out of the kieve, a mug out of the barrel, a pitcher out of the mug, a measure out of the pitcher, and a mether out of the measure. And I leave it to the great God' he said 'that I do not know where is their dust now, after the crumbling of them away from me through age.'

HOW CONCHUBAR THE HIGH KING DIED FOR CHRIST

The time Conchubar High King of Ireland was fighting in Connacht and was given a wound in the head with a hard ball that lodged there, it was Fintain the great healer tended him, and took a thread of gold that was the one colour with the King's hair and sewed up the wound. And he bade him to be careful and not to give way to anger or to passion, and not to be running or to go riding on a horse. So through seven years he stayed in his quietness until the coming of the Friday of the Crucifixion. And on that day he took notice of a change that came over the world, and of the darkening of the sun until the moon was seen at the full; and he asked his druid that was with him the meaning of that great change. 'It is Jesus Christ the Son of God' said the druid 'that is

BOOK FIVE: GREAT WONDERS

at this time meeting with his death by the Jews. 'It is a pity' said Conchubar 'that he did not call out for the help of a High King. And that would bring me myself there' he said 'in the shape of a hardy fighter, my lips twitching, until the great courage of a champion would be heard breaking a gap of battle between two armies. It is with Christ my help would be; a wild shout going out; the keening of a full lord, a full loss. I would make my complaint to the trusty army of the high feats, their ready beautiful help would relieve him; beautiful the overthrowing I would give his enemies; beautiful the fight I would make for Christ that is defouled; I would not rest although my own body was tormented. Why would we not cry after Christ, he that is killed in Armenia, he that is more worthy than any worthy king ? I would go to death for his safety; it crushes my heart to hear the outcries and the lamentations!' And with that he took his sword and he rushed at an oakwood that was near at hand, and began to hack and to fell the trees; and it is what he said that if he could be among the Jews, that is the treatment he would give them. And from the greatness of the anger that gripped him, the old wound in his head burst open and the ball started

OF THE OLDEN TIME

from it and brought away the brain with it. And that is the way Conchubar King of Ireland met with his death.

THE WONDERS TOLD BY PHILIP THE APOSTLE THAT WAS CALLED THE EVER-LIVING TONGUE

In the old time the people used to be looking at the moon and at the sun and the rest of the stars, travelling and ever-travelling through the day, and at the flowing and ever-flowing of the world's wells and rivers, and at the sadness of the earth and the trance and the sleep of it with the coming of winter, and the rising of the world again with the coming of the summer. But it was all like a head in a bag to them or like living in a dark house, until such time as Philip the Apostle told the whole story of the making of heaven and earth at the great gathering in the east of the world. It is the way that gathering was, it lasted through the four seasons under nine hundred white golden-crowned canopies upon the hill of Sion. And five thousand nine hundred and fifty tower-candles and precious stones there were kindled and giving out light that there might be no hindrance from any sort of weather. Late now upon Easter Eve there was heard a clear voice that was speaking

BOOK FIVE: GREAT WONDERS

the language of the angels, and the sound of it was like the laughter of an army or like the outcry of a very big wind; and with that it was no louder than the talk of friend in the ear of friend, and it was sweeter than any music. That now was the voice of Philip the Apostle, for it was he was sent to tell out the story of the making of the world; and it is long he was speaking and these are some of the wonders that he told.

THE SEVEN HEAVENS As to the Seven Heavens that are around the earth, the first of them is the bright cloudy heaven that is the nearest and that has shining out of it the moon and the scattering of stars. Beyond that are two flaming heavens, angels are in them and the breaking loose of winds. Beyond those an ice-cold heaven, bluer than any blue, seven times colder than any snow, and it is out of that comes the shining of the sun. Two heavens there are above that again, bright like flame, and it is out of them shine the fiery stars that put fruitfulness in the clouds and in the sea. A high heaven, high and fiery, there is above all the rest; highest of all it is, having within it the rolling of the skies, and the labour of music, and choirs of angels. In the belts now of the seven heavens are hidden the

OF THE OLDEN TIME

twelve shaking beasts that have fiery heads upon their heavenly bodies and that are blowing twelve winds about the world. In the same belts are sleeping the dragons with fiery breath, tower-headed, blemished, that give out the crash of the thunders and blow lightnings out of their eyes.

THE SECRETS OF THE SEA There are three waters of the sea now around the world. The first of them is a seven-shaped sea under the belly of the world, and against that sea hell is roaring and raising up a shout in the valley. The second is a sea green and bright round about the earth on every side; ebbing and flood it has and casting up of fruits. The third sea is a sea aflame, nine winds are let out of the heavens to call it from its sleep; three score and ten and four hundred songs its waves sing, and it awakened; a noise of thunder comes roaring out of its wave-voice; flooding and ever flooding it is from the beginning of the world, and with all that it is never full but of a Sunday. In its sleep it is till the thunders of the winds are awakened by the coming of God's Sunday from heaven, and by the music of the angels. Along with those there are many kinds of seas around the earth on every side; a red sea having many precious stones,

BOOK FIVE: GREAT WONDERS

bright as blood, well coloured, golden, between the lands of Egypt and the lands of India. A sea bright, many-sanded, of the colour of snow, in the north around the islands of Sabarn. So great is the strength of its waves that they break and scatter to the height of the clouds. Then a sea waveless, black as a beetle; no ship reaching it has escaped from it again but one boat only by the lightness of its going and the strength of its sails; shoals of beasts there are lying in that sea. A sea there is in the ocean to the south of the island of Ebian. At the first of the summer it rises in flood till it ebbs at the coming of winter; half the year it is in flood it is, and half the year always ebbing. Its beasts and its monsters mourn at the time of its ebbing and they fall into sadness and sleep. They awake and welcome its flooding, and the wells and the streams of the world increase; going and coming again they are through its valleys.

FOUR OF THE WORLD'S WELLS   The well of Ebian turns to many colours in the course of every day. The colour of snow is in it from the rising of the sun to tierce; green it is, many-changing like serpents, from tierce to nones. From nones to dawn it is turned to the colour of blood; no smile or laughter

OF THE OLDEN TIME

comes upon the mouth that has tasted it for ever. The well of Assian in Lybia gives help to barren women; drinking it they bear children. The well of Presens rises up against killers of parents, and idol worshippers, and all bad persons. Every mouth that tastes it turns to anger and madness and never speaks again, but perishes in grief and mourning. The well of Zion flows full on every Sunday; shining at night like the sun it is, and turning to every beautiful colour from holy hour to hour. There is no taste of oil or wine or honey in the world that is not found in it, and it never rests from filling and is never seen to flow away on any side. Sadness or trouble of mind has never come upon any one who has drunk of it, and he has not been given over to death.

THE FOUR PRECIOUS STONES The stone Adamant in the land of India grows no colder in any wind or snow or ice; there is no heat in it under burning sods; nothing is broken from it by the striking of axes and of hammers; there is one thing only breaks that stone, the Blood of the Lamb at the Mass; and every king that has taken that stone in his right hand before going into battle, has always gained

BOOK FIVE: GREAT WONDERS

the victory. The stone Hibien in the lands of Hab flames like a fiery candle in the darkness of the night. It spills out poison put before it in a vessel; every snake that comes near to it or crosses it dies on the moment. The stone of Istien in the lands of Lybia is found in the brains of dragons after their death. The pools and the great lakes boil up by reason of it over their borders; it shines through water; it is like thunder in the winter time but in summer it has the sound of the winds. The stone of Fanes in the lands of Aulol out of the stream of Dara. Twelve stars there are seen in its side and the wheel of the moon and the fiery journey of the sun. In the hearts of the dragons it is always found that make their journey under the sea. No one having it in his hand can tell any lie till he has put it from him. No race or army could bring it into a house where there is one that has made away with his father. At the hour of matins it gives out sweet music that there is not the like of under heaven.

THE FOUR TREES THAT HAVE A LIFE LIKE THE ANGELS   The tree Sames at the meeting of Jor and Dan bears its fruit three times every year. Bright green its first fruit is, and red the next, and the last

OF THE OLDEN TIME

is shining; when the first of the fruit is ripe another grows out of its flowers, and every witless person tasting that fruit comes back into his right mind. No leaf has ever fallen from that tree, and there is no person having sickness upon him or blemish, but is healed through coming under its shadow. The tree of Life in Adam's Paradise; no mouth that has tasted its fruit has gone to death afterwards, and it was by reason of that tree Adam and Eve were banished out of Paradise; for if they had tasted its fruit death would not have come to them at any time, but they would have been ever-living. Twelve times it bears fruit every year, in every month a well-coloured harvest; and the sweet smell of Paradise reaches out from it as far as a seven summer days' journey. The tree Alab in the islands of Sab is shaped in the form of a man; the blossoms of it quell every disease and every poison; the sweet smell of its flowers is felt to the length of a journey of six summer days; precious stones are the kernels of its fruit. Anger it banishes and envy it banishes from every heart that its juice has run over. The tree Nathaben in the lands of the Hebrews south of Mount Zion. That tree

BOOK FIVE: GREAT WONDERS

was never found by any son of men from the beginning of the world, but on the one day only when there was need of a tree for Christ's hanging; and it is from its branches the Cross was made through which the world was saved. Seven times it bears fruit in the year, and seven times it changes its flowers, and the brightness of the moon and of the sun and the shining of the stars shine out of them; and its leaves and its flowers sing together since the beginning of the world, two and seventy kinds of music at the coming of the winds. Three score birds and five and three hundred, bright like snow, golden-winged, sing many songs from its branches; it is a right language they sing together, but the ears of men do not recognise it.

THE JOURNEY OF THE SUN   God made on the fourth day the two and seventy kinds of the wandering stars of heaven, and the fiery course of the sun that warms the world with the sense and the splendour of angels. Twelve plains there are under the body of the earth he lightens every night; the fiery sea laughs against his journey; ranks of angels come together, welcoming his visit after the brightness of the night. The first place he brightens is the stream beyond the

OF THE OLDEN TIME

seas, with news of the eastern waters. Then he lightens the ocean of fire and the seas of sulphur-fire that are round about the red countries. Then he shines upon the troops of boys in the pleasant fields, who send out their cry to heaven through dread of the beast that kills thousands of armies under the waves of the south. Then he shines upon the mountains that have streams of fire, on the hosts that protect them in the plains. Then the ribs of the great beast shine, and the four and twenty champions rise up in the valley of pain. He shines over against the terrible many-thronged fence in the north that has closed around the people of hell. He shines on the dark valleys having sorrowful streams over their faces. He brightens the ribs of the beast that sends out the many seas around the earth; that sucks in again the many seas till the sands on every side are dry. He shines upon the many beasts that sleep their sleep of tears in the valley of flowers from the first beginning of the world; and on the sorrowful tearful plain, with the dragons that were set under the mist. He shines then upon the bird-flocks singing their many tunes in the flower-valleys; upon the shining plains with the wine-flowers that

BOOK FIVE: GREAT WONDERS

lighten the valley; he shines at the last against Adam's Paradise till he rises up in the morning from the east. There would be many stories now for the sun to tell upon his journey, if he had but a tongue to give them out.

THE NATURE OF THE STARS The stars now differ in their nature from one another. As to the ten stars of Gaburn, trembling takes hold of them, and fiery manes are put over their faces, to foretell a plague or a death of the people. Other stars there are that bring great heat or great cold or great mists upon the earth; others there are that run to encourage the dragons that blow lightnings on the world; others of them run to the end of fifty years and then ask their time for sleeping. To the end of seven years they sleep till they awake at the shout of the blessed angels, and the voices of the dragons of the valley. Others run through the six days and the six nights till the coming of the Sunday; at its beginning they begin their many kinds of music, and they fall asleep again till the coming again from heaven of God's Sunday, and with that they follow the same round.

THE HIGH EVER-LIVING BIRDS The birds of the island Naboth, it is a

OF THE OLDEN TIME

pleasant work they are doing; they give a welcome to the heat and to the colours of the summer; at midnight they awake and sing the sweet string-music; there never was seen upon the floor of the world any colour that is not upon their wings.

The birds of Sabes; their wings shine in the night-time like candles of fire; sickness is turned to health under the shadow of their wings; they fall into a sleep of darkness in the cold time of the winter; at the first of the summer they awake. They sing in their sleep a high pleasant song, that is like the thunder of wind.

The birds of Abuad in the islands between the east of Africa and the sky; their feathers have lasted on them from the very beginning of the world; there is not one bird of them wanting; there is no increase of their numbers. The sweet smell of the flowers, the taste of the seven wine-rivers of the plain where they have their dwelling, that is their lasting food; they sing their song in a right fashion, till the coming of the song of the angels in the night.

The three bird-flocks are divided; they give their share of music to the humming of the angels overhead; swift as riders on horses

BOOK FIVE: GREAT WONDERS

they travel quickly through the air. Two birds and seventy and seventy thousand and no lie in it, that is the number surely in every flock of the birds.

The first of the flocks sing pleasantly; it is not unfitting is their sweetness, the whole of the wonderful courses that God made before the world.

The birds that are well-wishers tell out in the end of the night-time all the wonders God will do in the day of the Judgement of the Racings.

If men could but hear those birds without fault giving out their pleasant talking, and ever to part with that music again, they would die with fretting after it.

FOUR OF THE STRANGE RACES OF MANKIND
As to the fighting-men of the island of Ebia, six and fifty feet is the length of every one of them. They do not awake out of their sleep but through a storm of the sea or the outcry of a battle or the sound of music; when they rise up out of sleep their eyes are shining like the stars. They conquer the seas by a hint from their eyes till the beasts of it cast themselves ashore to satisfy them. Fair flaming people in the island of Idab;

OF THE OLDEN TIME

flames come from their mouth in the weight of their anger; their eyes shine like candles in the night time; the hair and the bodies of them shine like snow smelted into great whiteness; fish from many seas, without boiling, without broiling, that is their provision. The women in the mountains of Armenia, their bodies are greater than those of any people; they bear daughters only; their anger and their courage as they go into battle is harder than the anger of men. They rise from their sleep at midnight, they loose flashes of fire from their mouths; their beards reach to their middle; there is always found in their right hand after birth, gold that is brighter than every blaze. The people of Fones in the lands of Lybia; their eyes flame like sparks of fire in their anger; there cannot come enough of men about one of them to put him down by force; the strength and the sweetness of their voices are above any voices and any horns; at the time of their dying it is a stream of wine that comes from their mouth; in their sleep they sing a mournful song, the like of it has not been found.

THE VALLEY OF PAIN   So great is the greatness of the cold there, that if a

BOOK FIVE: GREAT WONDERS

breath the like of it could be thrown into the world through the hole of a pipe, every bird in the air and every beast under the sea and everything living on the earth would die.
So great is the fierceness of the fire there, that if some of it should be cast into the world through a pipe, all the waters would ebb before it, and the living beasts in the sea would burn.
So great is the greatness of the hunger and thirst there, that if a share of it could be thrown into the world for one hour only, all that it would find of beasts and of men and of birds, would perish in that hour through hunger and through thirst.
So great is the greatness of the fear there, that if one grain of such fear should come into the world, all the creatures of the sea and of the air and the earth, would fall into madness and lose their wits through the dint of the terror, and would die.
Such is the greatness of the grief and the sorrow there, that if any of it could be cast through a pipe into the world, there would be no warmth, nor pleasure, nor faces of friends, nor wine, nor welcome; but every heart it came to would die under crying and under grief.

OF THE OLDEN TIME

It was Philip the Apostle told out these wonders and many others along with them to the kings and the people and the children at the great gathering in the east of the world.

THE CLOUD OF WITNESSES The time Mochaemhog, saint of the Gael, made his dwelling-place at Liath Mor, the King of Munster took a liking to a meadow belonging to him, and he put his horses into it; and when Mochaemhog got word of that he went and turned them out of the meadow. There was great anger on the King then, and he gave orders the saint should be banished out of the country. But when Mochaemhog heard that, he went straight to Cashel of the Kings, and he himself and the King of Munster disputed for a while. And after that in the night time the king had a vision, and in the vision an old man, very comely and shining, came to him and took him by the hand, and led him from the room to the wall of Cashel that was to the south side, and from it he saw the whole of Magh Femen filled with a host of white saints having the appearance of flowers. He asked what great host that was, and the old man said they were Blessed Patrick and the saints of Ireland that

BOOK FIVE: GREAT WONDERS

had come to the help of Mochaemhog. 'And if you do do not make an agreement with him' he said 'you will meet with your death.' The king fell asleep then, and he saw the old man coming to him a second time, and he took him by the hand again and led him to the wall on the north side. And from there he showed him a sight like the first, the whole of Magh Mossaid filled with a shining flowery host, having white clothing; and it seemed to the king that they stopped at the mering between the two plains. And the old man told him that was the host of Saint Brigit and all the holy young girls of Ireland, that were brought there by Blessed Ita, that was of the kindred of Mochaemhog and his fosterer.

A PRAISE OF CAILLEN AND HIS BLESSED DEATH

Caillen, saint of the Gael, told the whole story of Ireland from the very beginning. It was by Finntain the high elder of Ireland he was reared and taken care of until his hundredth year was at an end. He sent him then to the East the way he would bring back knowledge to the men of Ireland. And he stopped there in the East through the length of two hundred years.

OF THE OLDEN TIME

It was an angel brought him back to Ireland, to the Yew Tree at Baile's Strand to wear out the rest of his life. 'And the reason I stop here' he said 'in Ireland of many crosses, is that I never saw to this day a country that is more blessed.'

It was Caillen turned the druids into stone pillars because they mocked at the clerks; it is he was an unebbing sea in wonders and in lasting praise of his Master.

Columcille came and stopped with him a while at the place of Baile's Yew Tree. His choice place it was of all he had ever seen, north or east, south or west.

Conall King of Teamhuir put it on his children to pay tribute to Caillen and to them that came after him for ever; it is the tribute he promised, in the presence of the saints of Ireland, the riding horse of every king in every third year, and his coloured cloak; and a horse from the wife of every chief man. The sureties now of that tribute were Patrick apostle of Ireland with his saints, and Michael with the angels of heaven.

It was Patrick gave Caillen the bell that would heal every sickness and every oppression and trouble, and that brought to the sons of Niall that obeyed it fair weather, pros-

BOOK FIVE: GREAT WONDERS

perity and peace, and the good luck of a king in every place; & that bell was the breaking of luck to every troop it was rung against.

When God thought it time Caillen should go to heaven, and when the people of heaven were standing waiting for him, it is in the church he was of Mochaemhog, that had given baptism to the children of Lir.

And he told out a vision he had that night; 'And it vexed my heart and my head' he said 'for I saw in it the Saxons coming across the sea, and I saw Ireland in great bondage under them. And it is time for me to go to heaven' he said 'for I have fulfilled five hundred years to-night. And when my body is buried' he said 'there will be a host of angels near me. For three hundred angels there used to be about me at my rising and at my lying down in my bed; and I never said the Hours until such time as I heard the people of Heaven doing the like.'

Until now, the stars of the sky, and the sands of the sea, and the grass and the rest of the herbs of the earth, and the dew that is on them are counted, I could not tell all the wonders done by blessed Caillen, unless an angel of God would teach me.

OF THE OLDEN TIME

THE CALLING OF MARTIN THE MILLER There is blood shed in every house of the Gael in Ireland on Saint Martin's day, for he is a great saint and he has given good help to many a poor man. A miller he was, and the Blessed Mother and the Child came to him one time at the mill, and the Mother held out a few grains of wheat in her hand and she said 'Put those in the quern and turn the wheel for me.' 'It is no use' said he 'to put in a little handful of grains like that.' 'It is use' said the Blessed Mother. So he put them in the quern then and turned the wheel, and there were ten sacks in the place, and they were all filled with the flour that came from those few grains. And when Saint Martin saw that, he sold the mill and all that he had, and went following after the Blessed Mother and the Child.

MARTIN AND THE GRASS-CORN He went to a house one time, and the farmer that owned the house was out scattering water on the field, for there was red heat that year and no rain, and he had the seed sown and he did not think the corn would grow without he would go scattering water on it. The woman of the house told that to Saint Martin; and she was mixing dough at

BOOK FIVE: GREAT WONDERS

the time, and he asked a bit of the dough of her and she gave it, for he had the appearance of a poor man. And he put the bit of dough she gave him in the oven and went away leaving it there. And when the woman of the house opened the oven after a while, there was grass-corn growing up through the dough, and a drop of dew on the top of every blade. It was for an example Martin did that, to show the man of the house that God could make grass-corn grow even in the heat of the oven; for if he had believed that, he would not have gone scattering water over the fields.

THE BIRTH OF COLMAN OF AIDHNE   When Rhinagh that was of the race of Dathi was with child by Duach, it was told to the King of Connacht of that time that the son she would bear would be greater than his own sons. And when he heard that, he bade his people to make an end of Rhinagh before the child would be born. And they took her and tied a heavy stone about her neck and threw her into the deep part of the river, where it rises inside Coole. But by the help of God, the stone that was put about her neck did not sink but went floating upon the water, and she came to the shore and was saved from drowning. And that stone is to be seen yet,

OF THE OLDEN TIME

and it having the mark of the rope that was put around it. And just at that time there was a blind man had a dream in the north about a well beside a certain ash tree, and he was told in the dream he would get his sight if he bathed in the water of that well. And a lame man had a dream about the same well that he would find at Kiltartan, and that there would be healing in it for his lameness. And they set out together, the lame man carrying the man that had lost his sight, till they came to the tree they had dreamed about. But all the field was dry, and there was no sign of water unless that beside the tree there was a bunch of green rushes. And then the lame man saw there was a light shining out from among the rushes; and when they came to them they heard the cry of a child, and there by the tree was the little baby that was afterwards Saint Colman. And they took him up and they said 'If we had water we would baptize him.' And with that they pulled up a root of the rushes, and a well sprang up and they baptized him; and that well is there to this day. And the water in springing up splashed upon them, and the lame was cured of his lameness, and the blind man got his sight. And many that would have their blindness cured go and sleep beside that

BOOK FIVE: GREAT WONDERS

well; and many that are going to cross the sea to America, take with them a bit of a blessed board from an old tree that is in that field.

HIS HOME IN BURREN   He was a great saint afterwards, and his name is in every place. Seven years he was living in Burren in a cleft of the mountains, no one in it but himself and a mouse. It was for company he kept the mouse, and it would awaken him when he was asleep and when the time would come for him to be minding the Hours. And it is not known in the world what did the dear man get for food through all that time. And that place he lived in is a very holy place, being as it is between two blessed wells. No thunder falls on it, or if there is thunder it is very little, and does no injury.

THE LITTLE LAD AND THE BIRDS   And if it is long since Colman left this life and the churches he had made, it is well he minds the people yet, and there are many get their eyesight at the wells he blessed, and it is many a kindness he has done from time to time for the people of Aidhne and of Burren. There was a little lad in Kiltartan one time that a farmer used to be sending out to drive the birds off his crops; and there came a day that was very hot and he was tired, and he dared not go in or fall asleep, for he was in dread of the farmer beating him. And he prayed to Saint Colman, and the saint came and called the birds into a barn, and they all stopped there through the heat of the day till the little lad got a rest, and never came near the grain or meddled with it at all.

THE LITTLE LAD IN THE WELL There was a boy fell into the blessed well that is near the seven churches at Kilmacduagh, a little lad he was at the time, wearing a little red petticoat and a little white jacket. And when some of the people of the house went to draw water, they looked down in the well and saw him standing up in the water, and they got him out and brought him in to the fire and he was nothing the worse. And he said it was a little grey man, that was Saint Colman, came to him in the well and put his hand under his chin, and kept his head up over the water.

COLMAN HELPS A FARMER There was a man going home from Kinvara one night having a bag full of oats on the horse. And it fell and he strove to lift it again but he could not, for it was weighty. Then the saint himself, Saint Colman, came and helped

BOOK FIVE: GREAT WONDERS

him with it, and put it up again for him on the horse.

HE SHOWS RESPECT FOR RESPECT There was another man living up beyond Corcomruadh, and he never missed to go to the blessed well that is above Oughtmana on the name day of the Saint. And at last it happened he was sick in his bed and he could not go. And Saint Colman came to him to the side of the bed and said 'It is often you came to me, and now it is I myself am come to you.' It is about forty years ago that happened.

A VERY GOOD WELL Saint Colman's well beyond Kinvara is a very good well. To perform around it seven times you should, and to leave a button or a tassel or some such thing on the bush. The people of Coole and of Tyrone used to be going to it at the time of the wars, asking safety for their sons and their husbands and their brothers. And whoever would pray there would be freed from the war, and would come safe home again.

MARBHAN'S HYMN OF CONTENT Marbhan that was brother to Guaire King of Connacht, left his brother's house and his share of his father's inheritance, and went into some lonely wild place, it is likely

OF THE OLDEN TIME

in some part of Burren, where Colman that was his kinsman had gone. And some say he was herding pigs for the King there, but anyway he was serving God. And King Guaire followed him there and asked him to come back where he could sleep upon a bed and not be laying his head upon a hard fir tree in the night time. But Marbhan would not leave the place he had chosen, for he said he was well content with the little cabin he had in the wood, and that no one had knowledge of except God. And he made a song praising it and it is what he said:

'The size of my cabin is small, not too small; it is many are its lucky paths; a beautiful woman, coloured like a blackbird, sings a sweet strain upon the roof.

'Goats and swine are lying down about it; tame pigs, wild pigs, grazing deer; a badger's brood, foxes to meet them in peace, that is delightful.

'An apple tree, great the advantage, ready like an inn, lucky; a thick little bush with fistfuls of hazel-nuts; green, full of branches.

'A rowan tree, a sloe bush; dark black thorns, plenty of food; acorns, haws, yew berries; bare berries, bare flags.

'Buzzing of bees, the heifers lowing, the

BOOK FIVE: GREAT WONDERS

cackle of wild geese before the winter; the voice of the wind against the branches; that is delightful music.

'And in the eyes of Christ' he said 'I am no worse off than yourself Guaire, without one hour of fighting or the noise of quarrels in my house.' And when Guaire heard that he said he would be willing to give up his inheritance and his kingship to be in the company of Marbhan.

GUAIRE, THE HELPER OF THE POOR For if Guaire was not a saint, he was well worthy to be the brother and the kinsman of saints, and they would never have been in poverty if he had his way. And he gave alms till his right arm grew to be longer than the left, with the dint of stretching it out to the poor. He was beaten in battle one time by Diarmuid Ruanaidh, and he had to make his submission, lying stretched on the ground, and having the point of Diarmuid's sword beneath his teeth. And when he was lying that way Diarmuid said 'We will find out now is it for the love of God he does his great charity, or is it for the praises of the people.' So he bade a poor miserable beggar of his people to ask an alms of Guaire. 'An alms to me Guaire!' said the

OF THE OLDEN TIME

beggar; and Guaire gave him his golden pin. The beggar went from him then, but a man of Diarmuid's people followed him and took away the pin and gave it to Diarmuid. Then the beggar came back to Guaire, complaining and telling how the pin was taken from him. And there was pity in Guaire's heart and he gave him his belt that had on it golden ornaments, and that was all he had left to him of riches, and the beggar went away, and Diarmuid's people followed him the second time and took away the belt and gave it to Diarmuid. Then the beggar came back with his story to Guaire where he was lying, having the sword between his teeth yet. And when King Guaire saw the poor man so sorrowful, great tears went rolling down his cheeks. Diarmuid asked him then 'Is it for being conquered by me you are in that trouble?' 'I give my word' said Guaire 'it is not, but it is for the sake of that beggar over there.' And Diarmuid said 'Rise up, it is not under my power you should be, or to me you should show submission, for you are under the power of a king that is better than myself, the King of heaven and earth.'

HIS KINDNESS TO THE BUSH   One time there was a great troop of the poets

BOOK FIVE: GREAT WONDERS

in Guaire's house in the winter time, and a woman of the poets' household had a desire for ripe blackberries. But everybody said there were no blackberries to be got, ripe or unripe, at that time of the year. But as one of Guaire's people was out in the fields he saw a bush that was covered with a cloak, and under the cloak the blackberries were ripe and sound, and they were brought in to the woman, and there was no reproach upon the King's house. This now was the way that happened: King Guaire was going through the field at harvest time, and the thorns of the bush took hold of the cloak he was wearing, and held it. And Guaire was not willing to refuse so much as a bush that asked anything of him, and he left the cloak there on the branches. And for that kindness he got his reward in the end.

THE MAKING OF THE HARP   It was Marbhan the hermit that gave out news one time of the way the first harp was ever made, and this is the story that he told. There was a man and his wife, Cuil son of Midhuel the man was, and Canoclach was the name of the wife. And she took a hatred to her husband, and she was running from him through every wilderness and every wood, and he was following after her ever and always. One day now the woman came to the sea at Camas, and she was walking along the strand and she met with the bare bones of a whale, and she heard the sounds of the wind passing through the bones and the sinews, and with listening to those sounds she fell asleep. And her husband came there and saw her sleeping, and when he knew it was through those sounds that sleep had fallen upon her, he went on into a wood and he made a shape like the hard high breast-bone of a crane, and he put strings into it of the sinews of the whale; and that was the first harp of all the harps of the world.

MOCHAE AND THE BIRD   It was on the Island of One Ridge on Loch Cuan that Mochae the Beautiful, saint of the Gael, built his church and the dwelling of the brothers. He went out, now, one day, and seven score young men with him, cutting rods to build the church, and he himself was working like the rest of them. He had his load ready before the others and he sat down beside it; & just then he heard a bird singing on the branch of a blackthorn that was close at hand; and it was more beautiful than any of the birds of the world. 'This is

BOOK FIVE: GREAT WONDERS

hard work you are doing, Clerk' it said. 'That is required of me in building a church of God' said Mochae. 'And who is it is speaking to me?' he said. 'It is an angel of God is here' said the bird 'one of the people of Heaven.' 'A welcome to you and for what cause are you come?' 'To speak the word of God and to cheer you for a while.' 'That pleases me well' said Mochae. Then the little bird from Heaven sang to Mochae three songs from the tree where he was, and there was fifty years in each song of those songs. And Mochae stopped there listening to it through three times fifty years, in the middle of the wood and having his bundle of rods by his side, and they were not withered, and the time seemed to him as if it was but one hour of the day. Then the angel left him and Mochae went back to the church with his load, and there he found a house of prayer that had been built to his memory by his friends, and he wondered at seeing a church built there. And when he came to the house where the brothers were, there was no one in it that knew him. But when he told his story and the way the bird had sung to him, they all knelt before him and made a shrine with the rods he had carried. And after that they

OF THE OLDEN TIME

built a church on the spot where he had listened to the bird; and the walls of that church are standing yet.

THE PRIEST THAT WAS CALLED MAD   There was a miller of Connacht more than fifty years ago, and he had his mill near the roadside. And the people do be saying there came some man that was no right man to him one night, and asked him would he sooner his wife or his son to lose their wits. The miller made little of that question 'For as to my wife' he said 'she is the most sensible woman in the whole parish, and as to my son, he is in the college now and within a week he will be a priest, and there is no danger of madness upon him.' 'Time is a good story-teller' said the stranger. The first Sunday now the son that had been made a priest came home he read the Mass, that was the first and the last that ever he read. For that very night madness came upon him and he stripped off every bit of clothing, and out and away with him through the country, and he bare naked, and carrying on his head a very large book he himself had written in Irish and in Latin. He quieted after that, but nothing anyone could do would bring him back to the father's house, and he would use

BOOK FIVE: GREAT WONDERS

nothing but a bit of meal or of watercress. And every night he would go and sleep alone in the mill, and having but the big book under his head. And in the daytime it was his custom to go out to a wide field where there was a great flock of sheep and of lambs, and he used to sit down in the middle of the field, and there was not a sheep or a lamb but would gather to him, and he used to be reading to them out of his book until he would be tired. Then everyone of them would come to him and would be licking his hands. And one time some person was listening to him unknown, and could hear him giving out his sermon to the sheep. 'Listen to me' he was saying to them 'you that are without sin. You are under the care of God, and there is grass growing for you and herbs, and there are nice white dresses upon you to keep you dry and warm; and there is no Judgement upon you after your death, and you are happier by far than the children of Eve.' And he told them of the coming of the Son of God to the earth, and the bad treatment and the abuse that he was given; and a great many other things he told them out of the book. One night late now his father was uneasy about him, and he got a

OF THE OLDEN TIME

lantern and went to the mill and another man along with him. And when they opened the door they saw the whole of the mill lit up as bright as if it was the sun was lighting it. And the mad priest was lying there in his sleep, and the big book under his head, and a great shining ram was standing on each side of him, guarding him.

THE OLD WOMAN OF BEARE

Digdi was the name of the Old Woman of Beare. It is of Corca Dubhne she was and she had her youth seven times over, and every man that had lived with her died of old age, and her grandsons and great-grandsons were tribes and races. And through a hundred years she wore upon her head the veil Cuimire had blessed. Then age and weakness came upon her and it is what she said:

'Ebb-tide to me as to the sea; old age brings me reproach; I used to wear a shift that was always new; to-day I have not even a cast one.

'It is riches you are loving, it is not men; it was men we loved in the time we were living.

'There were dear men on whose plains we used to be driving; it is good the time we passed with them; it is little we were broken afterwards.

BOOK FIVE: GREAT WONDERS

'When my arms are seen it is long and thin they are; once they used to be fondling, they used to be around great kings.

'The young girls give a welcome to Beltaine when it comes to them; sorrow is more fitting for me, an old pitiful hag.

'I have no pleasant talk; no sheep are killed for my wedding; it is little but my hair is grey; it is many colours I had over it when I used to be drinking good ale.

'I have no envy against the old, but only against women; I myself am spent with old age, while women's heads are still yellow.

'The stone of the kings on Feman; the chair of Ronan in Bregia; it is long since storms have wrecked them, they are old mouldering gravestones.

'The wave of the great sea is speaking; the winter is striking us with it; I do not look to welcome to-day Fermuid son of Mugh.

'I know what they are doing; they are rowing through the reeds of the ford of Alma; it is cold is the place where they sleep.

'The summer of youth where we were has been spent along with its harvest; winter age that drowns everyone, its beginning has come upon me.

'It is beautiful was my green cloak, my king

OF THE OLDEN TIME

liked to see it on me; it is noble was the man that stirred it; he put wool on it when it was bare.

'Amen, great is the pity; every acorn has to drop. After feasting with shining candles, to be in the darkness of a prayer-house.

'I was once living with kings, drinking mead and wine; to-day I am drinking whey-water among withered old women.

'There are three floods that come up to the dun of Ard-Ruide: a flood of fighting-men, a flood of horses, a flood of the hounds of Lugaidh's Son.

'The flood-wave and the two swift ebb-tides; what the flood-wave brings you in, the ebb-wave sweeps out of your hand.

'The flood-wave and the second ebb-tide; they have all come as far as me, the way that I know them well.

'The flood-tide will not reach to the silence of my kitchen; though many are my company in the darkness, a hand has been laid upon them all.

'My flood-tide! It is well I have kept my knowledge. It is Jesus Son of Mary keeps me happy at the ebb-tide.

'It is far is the island of the great sea where the flood reaches after the ebb; I do not

BOOK FIVE: GREAT WONDERS

look for flood to reach to me after the ebb-tide.

'There is hardly a little place I can know again when I see it; what used to be on the flood-tide is all on the ebb to-day!'

BOOK SIX:
THE VOYAGE OF BRENDAN

HIS VISION OF THE LAND OF PROMISE It is a monk going through hardship Blessed Brendan was, that was born in Ciarraige Luachra of a good father and mother. It was on Slieve Daidche beside the sea he was one time, and he saw in a vision a beautiful island with angels serving upon it. And an angel of God came to him in his sleep and said 'I will be with you from this out through the length of your lifetime, and it is I will teach you to find that island you have seen and have a mind to come to.' When Brendan heard those words from the angel he cried with the dint of joy, and gave great thanks to God, and he went back to the thousand brothers that were his people.

THE NEWS OF THE HIDDEN COUNTRY It happened now there was a young man by name Mernoke that was a brother in another house, and that went out in a ship looking for some lonely place where he might serve God at will. And he came to an island that is convenient to the Mountain of Stones, and he liked it well and stopped there a good while, himself and his people. But after that he put out his ship again and sailed on east-

BOOK SIX: VOYAGE OF BRENDAN

ward through the length of three days. And it seemed to him on a sudden that a cloud came around them, the way they were in darkness the whole of the day, till by the will of our dear Lord the cloud passed away and they saw before them a shining lovely island. There was enough of joy and of rejoicing in that island, and every herb was full of blossom and every tree was full of fruit; and as for the ground it was shining with precious stones on every side, and heaven itself could hardly be better. There came to them then a very comely young man, that called every one of them by name and gave them a pleasant welcome; and he said to them 'It would be right for you to give good thanks to Jesus Christ that is showing you this hidden place, for this is the country he will give to his darlings upon earth at the world's end, and it is to this place He himself will come. And there is another island besides this one' he said; 'but you have not leave to go on to it or to have sight of it at all. And you have been here through the length of half a year' he said 'without meat or drink or closing your eyes in sleep.' They thought now they had not been the length of half an hour in that place, they had been so happy and so content. And he told them that was the first dwelling place of Adam and Eve, and there never came darkness there, and the name of it was the Earthly Paradise. Then he brought them back to their ship again and when they were come to it he vanished out of their sight, and they did not know where was it he went.

Then they set out over the sea again, and where they came to land was the place where Brendan was and his brothers, and they questioned Mernoke's people as to where they had been. 'We have been' they said 'before the gates of Paradise, in the Land of Promise, and we had every sort of joy there and of feasting, and there is always day in it and no night at all.' And their clothes had the sweetness of that place about them yet and the brothers said 'We are certain indeed you have been in that place, by the happy smile of you.' And when Brendan heard all these tidings he stood still for a while thinking with himself; and after that he went about among the brothers and chose out twelve of them that he thought more of than of all the rest; and he consulted them and asked an advice of them. 'Dear Father' they said 'we have left our own will and our friends

BOOK SIX: VOYAGE OF BRENDAN

and all our goods, and have come as children to you; and whatever you think well to do' they said 'we will do it.'

THE BEGINNING OF BRENDAN'S SEARCH So with that Brendan made his mind up to search out that place by the help of God; and he fasted forty days and did hard penance. And he made a very large ship having strong hides nailed over it, and pitch over the hides, that the water would not come in. And he took his own twelve with him and took his leave of the brothers and bade them good-bye. And those he left after him were sorry everyone, and two among them came when he was in the ship and begged hard to go with him. And Brendan said 'You have leave to sail with me; but one of you will be sorry that he asked to come.' But for all that they would go with him. Then they rowed out into the great sea of the ocean in the name of our Lord and were no way daunted at all. And the sea and the wind drove the ship at will, so that on the morning of the morrow they were out of sight of land. And so they went on through forty days and the wind driving them eastward.

TO THE LAND OF PROMISE

THE VERY COMELY HOUND And at the last they saw to the north a very large island having hard rocks on every side, and they sailed around it for three days before they could come near any place of landing; but at the last they found a little harbour, and landed every one. Then there came of a sudden a very comely hound and it fell down at Brendan's feet and bade him welcome in its own way. 'Good brothers' said Brendan 'there is nothing for us to be in dread of, for I know this is a Messenger to lead us into a right place.' Then the hound brought them into a great hall where there was a table having a cloth upon it, and bread and fish; and there was not one of them but was glad of that, and they sat down and eat and drank; and after their supper they found beds ready for them and they took their fill of sleep.

THE ISLAND OF SHEEP And on the morrow they went back to their ship and they sailed a long time on the sea before they could see any land. And at last they saw before them a very green island, and when they landed and looked about them they saw sheep on every side the whitest and the finest that ever were seen, for every

BOOK SIX: VOYAGE OF BRENDAN

sheep was the size of an ox. There came to them then a very well-looking old man and he gave them a kind welcome and he said 'This place you are come to is the Land of Sheep, and there is never winter here but lasting summer, and that is why the sheep are so large and so white, for the grass and the herbs are the best to be found in any place at all. And go on' he said 'till you come by the Grace of God to a place that is called the Paradise of Birds; and it is there you will keep your Easter.'

JASCONYE THE FISH Then they went into the ship again and it was driven by storms till they saw before them another little island, and the brothers went to land on it but Brendan stopped in the ship. And they put fish in a cauldron and lighted a fire to boil it, and no sooner was the fire hot and the fish beginning to boil, than the island began to quake and to move like a living thing, and there was great fear on the brothers and they went back into the ship leaving the food and the cauldron after them, and they saw what they took to be an island going fast through the sea, and they could notice the fire burning a long way off, that they were astonished. They asked Brendan

TO THE LAND OF PROMISE

then did he know what was that great wonder, and Brendan comforted them and he said 'It is a great fish, the biggest of the fishes of the world, Jasconye his name is, and he is labouring day and night to put his tail into his mouth, and he cannot do it because of his great bulk.'

THE PARADISE OF BIRDS They went on then to the westward through the length of three days, and very downhearted they were seeing no land. But not long after by the will of God they saw a beautiful island full of flowers and herbs and trees, and they were glad enough to see it and they went on land and gave thanks to God. And they went a long way through that lovely country, till they came to a very good well and a tree beside it full of branches and on every branch were beautiful white birds, so many of them there were that not a leaf hardly could be seen. And it was well for them to be looking at such a tree, and the happy singing of the birds was like the noise of Heaven. And Brendan cried for joy and he kneeled down and bade the Lord to tell him the meaning of the birds and their case. Then a little bird of the birds flew towards him from the tree and with the

BOOK SIX: VOYAGE OF BRENDAN

flickering of his wings he made a very merry noise like a fiddle, and it seemed to Brendan never to have heard such joyful music. Then the little bird looked at him and Brendan said 'If you are a Messenger tell me out your estate and why you sing so happily.' And it is what the bird said: 'One time we were every one of us angels, but when our master Lucifer fell from heaven for his high pride we fell along with him, some higher and some lower. And because our offence was but a little one' he said 'our Lord has put us here without pain in great joy and merriment to serve what way we can upon that tree. And on the Sunday that is a day of rest' he said 'we are made as white as any snow that we may praise him the better. And it is twelve months' he said 'since you left your own place, and at the end of seven years there will be an end to your desire. And through these seven years' he said 'it is here you will be keeping your Easter until you will come into the Land of Promise.' Then the bird took his leave of them and went back to his fellows upon the tree. It was upon an Easter Day now all this happened. Then all the birds began to sing the Vespers, and there could be no merrier music if God himself

TO THE LAND OF PROMISE

was among them. And after supper Blessed Brendan and his comrades went to bed; and they rose up on the morning of the morrow and the birds sang the matins and said the verses of the psalms, and sang all the Hours as is the habit with Christian men. And Brendan and his people stopped there for eight weeks till after the Pentecost; and they sailed back again to the Island of the Sheep, and there they got good provision and took their leave of the old man their Helper, and went back into their ship.

THE SILENT BROTHERHOOD   Then the bird of the tree came to them again and he said 'You will sail from this to an island where there are four and twenty brothers and you will spend your Christmas with those holy men;' and with that he flew back again to his comrades. Then Brendan and his people went out again into the ocean in the name of God; and the winds hurled them up and down, that they were in great danger and tired of their lives. And they were tossed about through the length of four months and they had nothing to be looking at but the sky and the waves. And at the last they saw an island that was a good way off, and they cried to Jesus Christ to bring them

BOOK SIX: VOYAGE OF BRENDAN

there; but the waves rose about them another forty days and they were loath to go on living. They came then to a little harbour and it was too narrow for the ship to go into it, so they cast the anchor and they themselves reached to the land. And they went searching the island and they found two wells, and the water of the one was bright and clear but the water of the other was as if stirred and muddy. And some of them were going to drink from the wells but Brendan bade them not to do it without leave. Then a comely old man came to them and gave them a fair enough welcome, and he kissed Brendan and he led them by many good wells till they came to a great Abbey. And there were in it to welcome them four and twenty brothers having royal cloaks woven of threads of gold, and a royal crown before them and candles on every side. And the Abbot came and kissed Brendan very humbly and bade him and his people welcome; and he led them into a beautiful hall and mixed them there among his own people. Then there came one that served them by the will of God and gave them plenty of meat and drink and set a good white loaf between every two, and

TO THE LAND OF PROMISE

white well-tasting roots and herbs, but they did not know what roots those were, and they drank the water of the good clear well they had first seen. Then the Abbot came and heartened them and bade them to eat and to drink their fill. 'For every day' he said ' our meat and drink is brought to our cellar by a strong man; and we do not know where it is brought from but that it is sent to us through God. And we have never provided meat or drink for ourselves' he said; 'four and twenty brothers we are, and every day of the week He sends us twelve loaves, and on every Sunday and on the day of Saint Patrick twenty-four loaves, and the bread that we do not use at dinner we use it at supper-time. And now at your coming our Lord has sent us forty-eight loaves that we may be merry together. And always twelve of us go to dinner' he said 'while another twelve of us serve the quire; and we are here these fourscore years and in this country there is no sickness or bad weather. And there are seven wax tapers in the quire' he said 'that have never been lighted by any man's hand, and that burn day and night at every hour of prayers and that have never wasted or lessened through these fourscore

BOOK SIX: VOYAGE OF BRENDAN

years.' After that Brendan went to the church with the Abbot, and they said the evening prayers together very devoutly. And Brendan saw beautiful woven stuffs, and chalices of clear crystal, and in the quire were twenty-four seats for the twenty-four brothers and a seat for the Abbot in the middle of them all. And Brendan asked the Abbot how long it was they had kept silence so well that no one of them spoke to the others, and the Abbot said 'Our Lord knows no one of us has spoken to another these fourscore years.' And when Brendan heard that he cried for joy and 'Dear Father' he said 'for the love of God let me stop along with you here.' 'You know well' said the Abbot 'you have no leave to do that, for has not our Lord showed you what you have to do, and that you will turn back to Ireland in the end?' And as Brendan was kneeling in the church he saw a bright angel that came in by the window and that lighted all the candles in the church, and went out by the window again to Heaven. 'There is wonder on me' said Brendan 'those candles to burn the way they do and never to waste.' 'Did you never hear' said the Abbot 'how in the old time Moses saw a bush that was burning

TO THE LAND OF PROMISE

from the top to the ground, and the more it burned the greener were the leaves? And let you not wonder' he said 'the power of the Lord to be as great now as ever it was.'

THE FEAST OF THE RESURRECTION And when Brendan had stopped there through Christmas and for Little Christmas, he bade good-bye to the Abbot and the brothers and went back to the ship with his people. And the sea tumbled them up and down that they were sorry enough until Palm Sunday, and with its coming they came again to the Island of Sheep, and they met there with the same old man as before, and he welcomed them a second time. And on Holy Thursday after supper he washed their feet and kissed them, and they stayed in that place till Easter Eve; and then at his bidding they set out and sailed to the place where the fish Jasconye was lying. And they found upon his back the cauldron they had left there a year ago, and they kept the Feast of the Resurrection there upon the fish's back. And they sang there their Matins and their Vespers and all their Masses, and the great beast stayed as still as any stone.

THE BIRD'S FORETELLING And when they had kept their Easter with great

BOOK SIX: VOYAGE OF BRENDAN

honour they went on to the island having the tree of birds. And the little bird gave them a good welcome and it is lively was the sound of his song. So they stopped there from Easter to Candlemas the same as the year before, very happy and content, listening to the merry service that was sung upon the tree. Then the bird told Blessed Brendan he should go back again for Christmas to the Island of the Abbey, and at Easter he should come hither again and the rest of the year he should be labouring in the great sea in trouble and in danger. 'And so it will be with you from year to year to the end of forty years' he said 'and then you will reach to the Land of Promise; and then through forty days you will have your fill of joy. And after that you will return to your own country' he said 'quite easily and without any annoy, and there you will end your life.' Then the Angel that was their helper brought all sorts of provision and loaded the ship and made all ready. So they thanked our Lord for his great goodness that he had showed them so often in their great need, and they sailed out into the sea among great storms.

THE DANGERS OF THE SEA   And soon there came after them a horrible

TO THE LAND OF PROMISE

great fish that was following their ship and that was casting up such great spouts of water out of his mouth that they had like to be drowned, and he was coming so fast that he had all but reached to them. Then they cried on Jesus Christ to help them in that great danger. And with that there came another fish bigger than the first out of the west, and made an attack on him and beat him and at the last made three halves of him and went away again as he came, and they were very glad and gave thanks to Jesus Christ. And after that again they were very downhearted through hunger, for all their food was spent. And there came to them then a little bird having with him a great branch full of red grapes, and they lived by them through fourteen days and had their fill. And when that failed them they came to a little island that was full of beautiful trees, and fruit on every bough of them. And Brendan landed out of the ship and gathered as much of that fruit would last them through forty days, and they went sailing and ever sailing through storm and through wind. And of a sudden there came sailing towards them a great monster and it made an attack upon them and on their ship and had like to

BOOK SIX: VOYAGE OF BRENDAN

have destroyed them, and at that they cried pitifully and thought themselves as good as dead. And then the little bird that had spoken with them from the tree at Easter time came at the monster and struck out one of his eyes with the first attack and the other eye with the second and made an end of him that he fell into the sea; and it is well pleased Brendan was when he saw that bird coming. Then they gave thanks to God, and they went on sailing until Saint Peter's Day, and they sang the service in honour of the Feast. And in that place the water was so clear that they could see to the bottom, and it was all as if covered with a great heap of fishes. And the brothers were in dread at the sight of all the fishes and they advised Brendan to speak softly and not to waken the fishes for fear they might break the ship. And Brendan said 'Why would you that have these two years kept the Feast of the Resurrection upon the great fish's back be in dread of these little fishes?' And with that he made ready for the Mass and sang louder than before. And the fishes awoke and started up and came all around the ship in a heap, that they could hardly see the water for fishes. But when the Mass was ended each one of them turned

TO THE LAND OF PROMISE

himself and swam away, and they saw them no more.

A BORDER OF HELL   For seven days now they were going on through that clear water, and there came a south wind that drove them on and they did not know where were they going. And at the end of eight days they saw far away in the north a dark country full of stench and of smoke; and as the ship drew near it they heard great blowing and blasting of bellows, and a noise of blows and a noise like thunder, the way they were all afeared and blessed themselves. And soon after there came one starting out all burning, and he turned away again and gave out a cry that could be heard a long way off. And with that there came demons thick about them on every side, with tongs and with fiery hammers, and followed after them till it seemed all the sea to be one fire; but by the will of God they had no power to hurt them. And then the demons began to roar and cry, and threw their tongs at them and their hammers, and then they turned from the ship with a sorrowful cry and went back to the place they came from. 'What are you thinking?' said Brendan 'was this a merry happening? And we will come here no more'

BOOK SIX: VOYAGE OF BRENDAN

he said 'for that was a border of hell, and the devil had great hopes of us but he was hindered by Jesus Christ.' Then the south wind drove them farther again into the north, and they saw a hill all on fire and like as if walled in with fire, and clouds upon it, and if there was much smoke in that other place, there was more again in this. Then one of the brothers began to cry and to moan and to say his time was come and that he could stay in the ship no longer, and with that he made a leap out of the ship into the sea and he cried and moaned so dolefully that it was a pity to hear him. 'My grief' he said 'my wretched life; for now I see my end and I have been with you in happiness and I may go with you no more for ever!'

A MOST WRETCHED GHOST   Then the wind turned and drove the ship southward through seven days, and they came to a great rock in the sea, and the sea breaking over it. And on the rock was sitting a wretched ghost, naked and in great misery and pain, for the waves of the sea had so beaten his body that all the flesh was gone from it and nothing was left but sinews and bare bones. And there was a cloth tied to his chin and two tongues of oxen with it,

TO THE LAND OF PROMISE

and when the wind blew, the cloth beat against his body, and the waves of the sea beat him before and behind, the way no one could find in any place a more wretched ghost. And Brendan bade him tell who was he in the name of God, and what he had done against God and why he was sitting there. 'I am a doleful shadow' he said 'that wretched Judas that sold our Lord for pence and I am sitting here most wretchedly; and this is not my right place' he said 'for my right place is in burning hell, but by our Lord's grace I am brought here at certain times of the year, for I am here every Sunday and from the evening of Saturday, and from Christmas to Little Christmas and from Easter to the Feast of Pentecost and on every feast day of Our Lady; for he is full of mercy. But at other times I am lying in burning fire with Pilate, Herod, Annas and Caiaphas; and I am cursing and ever cursing the time when I was born. And I bid you for the love of God' he said 'to keep me from the devils that will be coming after me.' And Brendan said 'With the help of God we will protect you through the night. And tell me what is that cloth that is hanging from your head' he said. 'It is a cloth I gave to a leper when

BOOK SIX: VOYAGE OF BRENDAN

I was on earth, and because it was given for the love of God, it is hanging before me. But because it was not with my own pence I bought it but with what belonged to our Lord and his brothers' he said 'it is more harmful to me than helpful, beating very hard in my eyes. And those tongues that you see hanging' he said 'I gave to the priests upon earth and so they are here and are some ease to me, because the fishes of the sea gnaw upon them and spare me. And this stone that I am sitting upon' he said 'I found it lying in a desolate place where there was no use for it, and I took it and laid it in a boggy path where it was a great comfort to those that passed that way; and because of that it comforts me now, and there are but few good deeds I have to tell of' he said. On the evening now of the Sunday there came a great troop of devils blasting and roaring and they said to Brendan 'Go from this, God's man, you have nothing to do here, and let us have our comrade and bring him back to hell for we dare not face our master and he not with us.' 'I will not give you leave to do your master's orders' said Brendan 'but I charge you by the name of our Lord Jesus Christ to leave him here this night until tomorrow.'

TO THE LAND OF PROMISE

'Would you dare' said the devils 'to help him that betrayed his master and sold him to death and to great shame?' But Brendan laid orders on them not to annoy him that night, and they cried out horribly and went away, and with that Judas thanked Blessed Brendan so mournfully that it was a pity to hear him. And on the morning of the morrow the devils came again and cried out and scolded at Brendan. 'Away with you' they said 'for our master the great devil tormented us heavily through the night because we had not brought him with us; and we will avenge it on him' they said 'and he will get double pains for the six days to come.' And then they turned and took away with them that wretched one, quailing and trembling as he went.

PAUL THE HERMIT   Then Brendan and his people sailed through the length of three days and three nights, and on the Friday they saw before them an island. And when Brendan saw it he began to sigh and to cry. 'Paul the hermit is in that island' he said 'and there he has been without meat or drink these forty years.' And when they had come to land that old hermit came to them and humbly welcomed them, and his body

BOOK SIX: VOYAGE OF BRENDAN

was bare, but for his hair and his beard that covered it. And when Brendan saw him he cried and he said 'Now I see one that lives the life of an angel rather than a man.' But Paul said 'You yourself are better than myself, for God has showed you more of his hidden things than to any other.' And he told them his own story and how he had been fed by an otter through forty years by the grace of God. And then the two blessed men parted from one another and there was sorrow enough in that parting.

A LUCKY JOURNEY   Then they went back to the ship and they were driven towards the south by a great wind through the forty days of Lent. And on Easter Eve they reached to their good Helper and he gave them good treatment as he had done before. And then he led them to the great fish and it was upon his back they said their Matins and their Mass. And when the Mass was ended the fish began to move and he swam out very far into the sea and there was great terror on the brothers when he did that and they being on his back, for it was a great wonder to see a beast that was the size of a whole country going so fast through the seas. But by the will of God the fish set them

TO THE LAND OF PROMISE

down in the Paradise of Birds sound and whole and left them there and went from them. And they were well pleased to be in that place and they spent their time there till after the Trinity as they had done before.

THE LAND OF PROMISE And after that they took their ship and sailed through forty days eastward. And at the end of the forty days there came a great shower of hail and then a dark mist came about them, and they were in it for a long time. Then their Helper came to them and said 'Let you be glad now and hearten yourselves for you are come to the Land of Promise.' Then they came out of the dark mist and they saw to the east the loveliest country that any one could see. Clear it was and lightsome, and there was enough in it of joy, and the trees were full of fruit on every bough, and the apples were as ripe as at harvest time. And they were going about that country through forty days and could see no end to it, and it was always day there and never night, and the air neither hot nor cold but always in the one way, and the delight that they found there could never be told. Then they came to a river that they could not cross, but they could see beyond it the country that had no

BOOK SIX: VOYAGE OF BRENDAN

bounds to its beauty. Then there came to them a young man the comeliest that could be, and he gave them all a welcome, and to Brendan he showed great honour and took him by the hand and said to him 'Here is the country you have been in search of, but it is our Lord's will you should go back again and make no delay, and he will show you more of his hidden things when you will come again into the great sea. And charge your ship with the fruit of this country' he said; 'and you will soon be out of the world for your life is near its end. And this river you see here is the mering' he said 'that divides the worlds, for no man may come to the other side of it while he is in life; and when our Lord will have drawn every man to him, and when every man will know him and be under his law, it is then there will be leave to see this country, towards the world's end.' Then Brendan and his comrades did not fast from the fruit, but brought away what they could of it and of precious stones, and put them in their ship and went away homewards, and sorry enough they were to go.

BRENDAN'S HOME-COMING And they sailed home in their ship to Ireland and it is glad the brothers they had left after

TO THE LAND OF PROMISE

them were to see them come home out of such great dangers. And as to Brendan he was from that time as if he did not belong to this world at all, but his mind and his joy were in the delight of heaven. And it is in Ireland he died and was buried; and that God may bring us to the same joy his blessed soul returned to!

NOTE

The Irish text of the greater number of the hymns and legends in this book has been published in the *Revue Celtique, Irische Texte, Zeitschrift Celtische Philologie, Eriu,* and elsewhere. From this text I have worked, making my own translation as far as my scholarship goes, and when it fails taking the meaning given by better scholars. The *Old Woman of Beare* and the verses taken from the *Hymn of Marbhan* differ very slightly from the translations published by Professor Kuno Meyer. I and my readers are indebted to the work of Mr. Whitley Stokes, especially in the *Voyage of Maeldune* (*Revue Celtique*) and the *Ever-Living Tongue* (lately published in full in *Eriu*), and to Mr. Standish Hayes O'Grady's inexhaustible *Silva Gaedelica*.

Among other Irish scholars and editors of texts to whom we owe thanks are O'Curry, O'Donovan, Reeves, Todd, Henebry, O'Donoghue, O'Beirne Crowe. Also to M. d'Arbois de Jubainville (*Cycle Mythologique*), Dr. Atkinson, and Rev. Dr. Bernard (*Liber Hymnorum*), Mr. Edward Gwynn (*The Priest and the Bees*), the

NOTE

Rev. M. O'Riordan (*Voyage of Brendan*), and to *An Craoibhin*.
I am grateful to these as well as to those men and women I have met in workhouses or on roadsides or by the hearth, who have kept in mind through many years the great wonders done among the children of the Gael.

NAMES OF PLACES STILL IDENTIFIED

Almhuin.	Hill of Allen, co. Kildare.
Ardmacha	Armagh.
Beinn Edair	Hill of Howth.
Boinne	The Boyne.
Beinn Gulbain	Near Sligo.
Bregia	Bray.
Carraige Luachra	Co. Kerry.
Corca Dubhne.	Corcaguiny, co. Kerry.
Cenacles.	Kells, co. Meath.
Cluain Eraird	Clonard.
Corcomruadh.	Near Burren, co. Clare.
Cruachan	Rathcroghan co. Roscommon.
Druimcliab	Drumcliff, co. Sligo.
Druim Ceta	The Mullagh, near Newtownards.
Doire	Derry.
Hill of Usnech.	West Meath.
Laighis	Leix.
Loch Lene	Killarney.
Loch Febhail	Lough Foyle
Loch Neach	Lough Neagh.
Magh Femen.	Near Sleve-na-Man.
Magh Breg	East Meath.
Moen	Moone, east of Athy.
Monaster Boite	Monasterboice, co. Louth.
Rathboth.	Between Donegal and Ballyshannon.

NOTE

Sord . . . Swords.
Sionnan . . . The Shannon.
Taillten . . . Telltown.
Toraig . . . Tory Island, co. Donegal.
Uaran Garaid . River Cruind.
Wood of Fochlad . North West of Sligo.

Printed in the United States
205182BV00001B/141/A